THE HEART OF A MARINE

BUILDING A LEGACY AFTER THE EXPLOSIONS HAVE STOPPED

JARED MCGOWEN

Lee -

Decide, take action
& commit!

Semper fi

THE **HEART** OF A **MARINE**

BUILDING A LEGACY AFTER THE EXPLOSIONS HAVE STOPPED

JARED MCGOWEN

WESTBOW
PRESS®
A DIVISION OF THOMAS NELSON
& ZONDERVAN

This book is a work of non-fiction. Unless otherwise noted, the author and the publisher make no explicit guarantees as to the accuracy of the information contained in this book and in some cases, names of people and places have been altered to protect their privacy.

WestBow Press books may be ordered through booksellers or by contacting:

WestBow Press
A Division of Thomas Nelson & Zondervan
1663 Liberty Drive
Bloomington, IN 47403
www.westbowpress.com
1 (866) 928-1240

Because of the dynamic nature of the Internet, any web addresses or links contained in this book may have changed since publication and may no longer be valid. The views expressed in this work are solely those of the author and do not necessarily reflect the views of the publisher, and the publisher hereby disclaims any responsibility for them.

Any people depicted in stock imagery provided by Getty Images are models, and such images are being used for illustrative purposes only. Certain stock imagery © Getty Images.

ISBN: 978-1-9736-4630-3 (sc)
ISBN: 978-1-9736-4629-7 (hc)
ISBN: 978-1-9736-4631-0 (e)

Library of Congress Control Number: 2018913814

Print information available on the last page.

WestBow Press rev. date: 11/29/2018

Lord, I'm not telling you anything you don't already know: I've never been a saint. Ever since I was a child, I've prayed to you, some years more than others, but one thing is for sure: I've seen firsthand the power you have. Throughout my service in the United States Marine Corps, you provided a force field around my entire battalion and me. When I replay some of the scenarios in my head, you're the only answer as to why we aren't guarding the gates of heaven right now. You have also blessed me with a woman who has inspired me to succeed in life and has given me three incredible children. Lyndsey and I are excited to say that we have accepted Jesus Christ into in our hearts as our Lord and Savior, confessed our sins, and are raising our children as faithful Christian leaders. Thank you!

To my wife, you're a champion! We met only eight months after I was discharged from the Marine Corps. I had just returned home from a devastating combat deployment in Iraq. I admit I was a ticking time bomb and unstable. You are a blessing from God, and I can honestly say with all my heart that you are the reason I'm not broke and in a bar today. I'm always striving to be a better husband and father than I was the year before; it's you who keeps me moving forward. Thank you for being you! And thank you to Gayle and Mark for making the woman of my dreams. I love you, Lyndsey!

My beautiful children, who can be sweet little angels one minute and make Mom and Dad lose their minds the next minute, you three are the reason I wake up every day and grind. The drive I have to succeed and create a legacy for our family is because of you. Every time I feel like quitting or slacking, I look at you and think of the lessons you are learning by watching my actions. I can only pray that when I'm old and gray and you each have a family of your own that you are valuable members of society and are making a difference in the world. I love you with all my heart!

To my mother, as I was growing up, we didn't have a lot of money. In fact, often we didn't have any. We never had the newest shoes, you cut our hair because it saved us money, and we were never able to go on fancy vacations. However, you kept our bellies full, and you loved us unconditionally. It's funny how I find myself saying the same things to my kids that you said to us. Oh, and thank you for telling me that my kids will act just like me one day, because they do. Thank you for always supporting me. I love you!

To the marines of Second Light Armored Reconnaissance (LAR) Battalion, throughout life, we make hundreds if not thousands of friends; some are considered close, whereas others are just acquaintances. No matter how close a friend or family member, there is nothing like the connection a marine feels to his or her comrades. Every single marine and sailor who served with Second LAR is closer than blood. It's been more than ten years since I've seen most of you, and we could reconnect right where we left off. We will forever be brothers, and I love you all. Thank you for making me who I am today!

Semper fi.

In Loving Memory

Lance Corporal Timothy Creager: killed in action on July 1, 2004.

Sergeant Chad Allen: killed in action on February 28, 2007.

CONTENTS

GLOSSARY OF ACRONYMS

AO	–	area of operation
CO	–	commanding officer
COP	–	combat outpost
CPL	–	corporal
DI	–	drill instructor
EOD	–	explosive ordnance disposal
FOB	–	forward operating base
Guide	–	head recruit
Head	–	bathroom
IED	–	improvised explosive device
LAR	–	light armored reconnaissance battalion
LAV	–	light armored vehicle
LCPL	–	lance corporal
LOD	–	line of departure
LZ	–	landing zone
MCRD	–	Marine Corps recruit depot
MRE	–	meal ready to eat
MSR	–	main supply route
NVG	–	night vision goggles
Oscar Mike	–	on the move
PFC	–	private first class
PSYOP	–	psychological operations
QRF	–	quick reaction force

Rack	–	bed
Rain room	–	shower room
ROE	–	rules of engagement
RPG	–	rocket-propelled grenade
SGT	–	sergeant
TCP	–	traffic control point
VC	–	vehicle commander

FOREWORD

The author, Jared McGowen, is a proven marine combat leader who has served in some of the most arduous and stressful situations a marine can find himself in. My relationship with Jared spans over fifteen years, including combat service together during Operation Phantom Fury in Fallujah, Iraq (2004–2005). He has proved himself to be an inspirational servant leader, giving entirely of himself and expecting nothing in return.

Jared has become highly successful as a civilian by incorporating the same skills that allowed him to excel as a marine. This transition is a difficult task faced by many American veterans every day as they depart the military. I have known and respected Jared since 2003, when we served alongside each other in Apache Company, Second Light Armored Reconnaissance Battalion, in Camp Lejeune, North Carolina. Jared has made it his life's mission to lead by example. In this endeavor, he aims to aid American citizens and particularly veterans by helping them find their purpose in life. His goal is for them to improve both personally and professionally. He desires to use the skills he acquired through the rigors of combat and his civilian life to motivate and inspire others to succeed.

As a marine and successful entrepreneur, Jared is an example of hard work and dedication for others to emulate. Let Jared's story of service—along with stories of other heroes he served with, which are depicted in *The Heart of a Marine*—be the impetus for your success. Let these heroes, who put it all on the line in service to this country, inspire you to be better Americans. Through Jared's unyielding spirit and desire to serve, his story can aid you in achieving your dreams. I have no doubts this book will inspire and assist the reader in building his or her legacy.

—Sergeant Major Bryan Link, USMC (Retired)

INTRODUCTION

This Is My Rifle

This is my rifle. There are many like it, but this one is mine. My rifle is my best friend. It is my life. I must master it as I must master my life. My rifle, without me, is useless. Without my rifle, I am useless. I must fire my rifle true. I must shoot straighter than my enemy who is trying to kill me. I must shoot him before he shoots me. I will … My rifle and myself know that what counts in this war is not the rounds we fire, the noise of our burst, nor the smoke we make. We know that it is the hits that count. We will hit … My rifle is human, even as I, because it is my life. Thus, I will learn it as a brother. I will learn its weaknesses, its strength, its parts, its accessories, its sights and its barrel. I will keep my rifle clean and ready, even as I am clean and ready. We will become part of each other. We will … Before God, I swear this creed. My rifle and I are the defenders of my country. We are the masters of our enemy. We are the saviors of my life. So be it, until victory is America's and there is no enemy, but peace!

—"Rifleman's Creed" by Marine Brigadier General William H. Rupertus

As a US Marine, I was part of the most feared fighting force in the world. If I wasn't at war, I was training for war. I could shoot a round through a flea at three hundred yards, my briefcase was a ruck pack, my rifle was my girlfriend, and my meals were packaged to last twenty-five years. I was trained to kill on more weapons systems than most people know exist. I had a vocabulary that would make a sailor blush and self-confidence that made people stare. Every day I'd wake up and breathe excellence while staring death in the face. I ran toward the sound of chaos; actually, I prayed for the sound of chaos. I had a saying. "Blood makes the grass grow; marines make the blood flow. Ready to fight, ready to kill, ready to die but never will."

My time as a US Marine consisted of some of the most tedious, miserable, exciting, and terrifying days of my life. However, the days of getting shot at were bound to come to an end eventually, so I hung up my boots and traded in my rifle for a laptop. I had a lot of questions.

- Now what am I supposed to do?
- I don't have to shave?
- Can I put my hands in my pockets?
- Can I walk and drink a beverage at the same time?
- What's a résumé?
- A suit? Can't I wear dress blues?
- Are you telling me I can't tell my coworkers to do push-ups? Can't I make them run laps for being late

to work? Their wrinkled clothes and long hair are acceptable?
- Are you telling me I need a college degree?
- Customer service—what's that?
- What's a CEO? Do you mean a CO or NCO?

Maybe I should reenlist!

The marine I just described was me when I left the US Marine Corps in 2007, but it's the life of thousands of other service members who return home and have no guidance or sense of direction when entering the civilian workforce. It's almost like we have been on another planet for years and speak another language. In the Marine Corps—specifically infantry—we are trained to accomplish one mission: locate, close with, and destroy the enemy. When my service ended, I was sent home with a certificate and a pat on the back. I was lost. I thought, *What do I want to do for a living? How do I translate my infantry skills to talents that will appeal to an employer?* These questions were heavy on my mind. I fought constant confusion and depression and covered it all up with long nights of drinking.

It's not only veterans who struggle to find their purpose; hundreds of thousands of other people also struggle to get ahead. Often, these people, such as me, were dealt a lousy hand in life. I was almost twenty-five when I finally figured out that it's not your fault if you're born into poverty; it is, however, your fault if you die in poverty.

In 2008, an encounter with a special woman changed the trajectory of my life. She had her long, blonde hair in a ponytail and was wearing basketball shorts but no makeup. I was a personal trainer at the time and was looking for a new client at the gym. After offering this beautiful young woman a free workout, the rest was history. We have been married eight years and have three beautiful children. I genuinely believe this introduction was a blessing from God, and I wouldn't be where I am today if it weren't for meeting my wife. I needed to change, and I needed a strong woman who could get my butt in gear. You'd better believe I gave her trouble along the way. After all, I'm a marine.

We all have our definitions of what a successful life is. For some, it's a loving family, a roof over their heads, and reliable transportation. For others, it may be excelling to the top ranks of their career fields and making a lot of money. Either way, you're right.

My mission is to teach, train, and inspire those looking to grow personally and professionally. I firmly believe that luck doesn't just happen; luck is when preparation meets opportunity. You are where you are today because of every decision you have made up to this point in your life. Ever since I was honorably discharged, I've held numerous positions for various companies that have led me to where I am today. I have a career that I love at a Fortune 25 company, and along with my wife, we have earned our way into the top 1 percent of a direct sales company. I've earned a bachelor's degree in marketing, a master's degree in business administration, and a master's degree in communications. And now I'm an author and speaker. The potential is within us all; it just needs to be unleashed with a plan of action and the drive to attack life with the confidence and the heart of a marine. People will get out of your way!

Four years as a marine infantryman produced more stories than I have time to write. And let's face it: I can't remember everything. I've been blown up way too many times. I'll be using letters I wrote to my family, journals I kept, and interviews with fellow marines to tell my story. My goal is to paint a picture of my experiences as a marine. You'll laugh, you might cry, and it's possible you'll feel some of the anxiety I felt along the way. After I take you on a journey down memory lane, I'll show you the principles I mastered that have helped me advance through life and leave the haters in the rearview mirror. I will also show you how I turned my experiences of death and destruction into fuel for my fire to not only succeed in life but also help others do the same.

PART 1
The Explosions

Some people spend an entire lifetime wondering
if they have made a difference in the world,
but the marines don't have that problem.

—RONALD REAGAN

CHAPTER
ONE

Eyeballs! Quick, Sir!

What did I get myself into? I thought at one o'clock in the morning as I loaded onto the bus and shoved my face into my lap, along with sixty other recruits from the San Diego airport. It seemed as if we drove around for hours, and the fear and uncertainty continued to grow. I was second-guessing my decision to join the marines. During this uncomfortable drive to the unknown, I reflected on my past and where I came from, realizing I had no clue what my future held. I had absolutely no military background. I mean, my grandfather had served in the navy, but he didn't talk much about it so I never heard any stories. College was out of the picture for me; my parents hadn't gone to college, and as I was growing up, education wasn't valued in our household. My options were limited.

"Marines Invade Iraq" was the headline of the newspaper I had opened a few months earlier, around March 2003. Before that moment, I had floated through life for almost a year after high school with two part-time, dead-end jobs.

I was stuck. When I read the headline, I felt a sense of pride for our country—and a sense of duty. And since September 11, 2001, was still fresh in my mind, I knew what I had to do. Seriously though, what nineteen-year-old kid looks at a newspaper picture of marines going to war and says, "I want to do that"? Maybe that's why I was a good fit. Later that day, I found myself at the recruiter's office. The following day, I was downtown testing. And less than three months later, there I was, my face in my lap and scared to move. *Wow, Jared, you thought this through.*

What was taking so long? Were they circling the airport? Just then, the bus came to a halt. I heard the old, squeaky door open, and footsteps climbed the stairs. The sound coming from the mouth of this drill instructor was scratchy. I could tell that this man yelled at the top of his lungs all day, every day.

"Sit up straight, and look at me! 'Aye, aye, sir!' Say it!"

"Aye, aye, sir!" we all shouted.

"On behalf of the commanding general, welcome to MCRD. You are now aboard Marine Corps Recruit Depot California, Receiving Company. From this point on, the only words out of your mouth are 'Yes, sir,' 'No, sir,' and 'Aye, aye, sir.' You will respond yes or no when someone asks a question. When I tell you to do something, that is an order, and you respond with 'Aye, aye, sir!' When you are speaking to a female, you will address her as ma'am. Do you understand that?"

"Yes, sir!"

There are columns of yellow footprints outside this bus. When we exit, you will move as fast as you can and stand on one. Your eyes will remain forward and your mouth shut.

Now without hurting yourself or anyone around you, get off my bus!"

The next seventy-two hours became a blur. It was a lot of "Hurry up and wait at the position of attention." "Toss everything you brought with you into the trash, and hurry up and wait." "Get a haircut in 2.2 seconds, and hurry up and wait." "Get naked in front of everyone, shove your civilian clothes in a bag, and hurry up and wait." "Get dressed on command, fill out paperwork, get assembly line vaccinations, and hurry up and wait."

The call home was quick. "Mom, this is Recruit McGowen. I have arrived safely at MCRD San Diego. You will receive a letter from me in the next week with more details about how to plan for graduation. I have to go now. Bye."

It must have been twenty-four hours before the drill instructors let us use the head, which is better known as the restroom. I was certain my bladder was going to explode. Plus I had never tried to urinate on command or share a toilet with four other men, so I had a severe case of stage fright. I couldn't go, and the time was up. About forty-eight hours in, we were finally able to hygiene. Now at this point, I had to poop really bad. Well, guess what. We hadn't earned toilet paper yet. Imagine that!

Over the next seven days in the receiving company, we prepared to officially start training and meet the drill instructors who would be with us twenty-four seven until graduation day. During that week, I couldn't help but think of home. I was scared to death, but I knew to become a marine would be the most significant accomplishment of my life. Here is the first letter I wrote home.

May 21, 2003

Family,

It's me! I have to hurry up and write this because I'm supposed to be sleeping. We finally get the opportunity to relax; over the last fifty hours, we have slept for only about three of them. I've had to hold going pee for over twenty-four hours, and I still haven't gotten a chance to poop. That probably won't be until Friday. Today is Wednesday night, May 21.

The first couple of days, I thought, *What in the world am I doing here?* This place is crazy; everything is *hurry up and wait*. I have to stand in line at the position of attention for sometimes three hours; it's painful. It's hot here, and we wear long sleeves and long pants along with our cover (hat) every time we are outside. The mess hall is nuts; we get in, eat, and get out into formation. The drill instructors are messed up. They constantly yell at the top of their lungs. Luckily, I haven't gotten singled out yet like many of the other recruits. This first week is pretty much miserable, but I keep my head straight and stay motivated. I'm a McGowen, and I will never quit. All I keep thinking about is graduation; it keeps me intense and motivated.

We finally got to shower today, and then we had to put on the same nasty clothes that we've been wearing since Monday morning. You should smell some of these guys. Friday, we get to meet our final senior drill instructor. They are not nice, if you know what I mean. Well, I better get to sleep. Or as the drill instructors would say, "Get up on your racks, you nasty civilians." I love you all, and I miss you!

In receiving week, we didn't have access to buy stamps yet, and I didn't want to get in trouble for dropping a letter in the mailbox, so I mailed this letter a week later.

The following day, we carried all our gear to our new squad bay, sat cross-legged, covered and aligned on the quarterdeck, and then waited on our drill instructors. The quarterdeck is a large, open area in the front of the squad bay, just outside the drill instructors' office. As we were waiting, perfectly still, I could see a DI in the corner of my eye.

"Eyeballs!" he shouted.

That was our cue to snap our heads toward him and say, "Quick, sir!"

He shouted again. "Ears!"

We responded with "Open, sir!"

Welcome to Black Friday!

CHAPTER

TWO

Make It Rain

B lack Friday. Don't get this confused with the shopping day created by retailers. Marine Corps Black Friday—otherwise known as Training Day 1—is the day when new recruits get placed with their final drill instructors. After a brief introduction by the series commander and the senior drill instructor, we were finally turned over to our three drill instructors, known as kill hats. Imagine this: you're at the zoo, the zookeeper puts three lions into a small fenced area with sixty gazelles, and there is no way out. That's about as accurate of a description of Black Friday as I can give. It was a nightmare of flipped racks, tossed seabags, dumped water, and thousands of push-ups, mountain climbers, burpees, puking recruits, and lost voices. Welcome to Third Battalion, Mike Company, Platoon 3095.

Boot camp was a wake-up call for me. I had always been a talented athlete with excellent physical conditioning; however, physical fitness is just a small piece of the pie, for the mind is what makes a marine. If you were the fastest runner, they would make you run until you couldn't run anymore. If you were the strongest, they would make you do push-ups until you fell on your face. No matter who you were, where you came from, or whether you were black, white, or Hispanic, or Christian, Catholic, or Jewish, you were beaten down mentally and physically.

One of the tasks taught to us the first night was how to shower properly. Picture this: We're sixty hot, sweaty, nasty recruits who have been wearing the same clothes for a week, and we line up in front of our racks. On command, we take off the articles of clothing as instructed. But wait. Someone didn't move fast enough, so we have to put everything back on. Once everyone is naked and standing in the wide-open squad bay, we run like a herd of sheep into the rain room, which is better known as the shower room. Sixty men are shoved into this rain room with sixteen shower heads and told to get wet. On command, we are to wash the part of the body as instructed, followed by rinsing off when told. Keep in mind that sixty recruits are attempting to do this while the drill instructors are yelling at the top of their lungs. At this moment, I had to let it all hang out; privacy didn't exist at MCRD San Diego.

For the next four weeks, our training schedule was consistent. Reveille would sound at 0500, lights were flipped on, and the drill instructors stormed out of their office with a mission to destroy us. We had 1.5 seconds to line up at the foot of our racks while wearing nothing but our tighty-whiteys and our skivvy shirts, ready to count off. Once everyone was present and accounted for, it was game on. Getting dressed wasn't like it was at Mama's house. The mental games didn't stop.

"Put your trousers on right now!" ("Aye, aye, sir!")

"Put your blouse on right now!" ("Aye, aye, sir!")

"Ten, nine, eight, seven, six, five, four, three, two, one, *zero!*"

Zero was our cue to freeze in our tracks and scream, "Freeze, recruit, freeze!"

"Good, you want to move slow?"

"Take your blouse off right now!"

"Take your trousers off right now!"

"Oh great. Dummy over here can't follow simple orders!"

"Everyone in the head *right now!*"

"Want to move slow? Fine. Back on line, right now!"

Mind games were how we started our morning routine. The goal was for them to create chaos for the simplest tasks. At first, your brain shuts down, and you have a hard time functioning. After a while, however, it becomes just part of our routine. The massive chaos was to help prepare us for combat. As marines, we have to stay focused for when chaos ensues and our buddy's leg gets blown off and we're pinned down by machine gun fire. Once we finally get dressed, usually within sixty to ninety seconds of waking up, we are given about thirty seconds to make our rack. Again, under extreme pressure, your sheets had better be pulled tight, with a perfect six-inch fold on top with forty-five-degree folds on the sides. On a few special occasions, the drill instructors didn't think we were moving fast enough, or there was a rack that wasn't to their standards. In this case, they would make everyone strip their blanket and sheets and start from scratch. Once the countdown was over, pending all racks looked tight, we trampled each other to get a quality angle on either a urinal or toilet. The standard rule was three recruits to a urinal and four to a toilet. No matter what, we always ran out of time. Don't even think about brushing your teeth, because we had thirty seconds to run down three flights of stairs out to the street to get into formation for morning chow. We visited the chow hall three times per day: breakfast, lunch, and dinner.

In a four-column formation, we marched to chow while the drill instructor called cadence. Once in the chow hall, it was a race to the finish. Time started when the last recruit sat down with his food, which was usually the guide (head recruit). While eating chow, we had to sit up straight with one hand on our knee and the other holding our utensil, heels at a forty-five-degree angle and head forward, and you'd better not get caught talking with someone at your table or accidentally make eye contact with a drill instructor. To drink, we had to grasp the cup with both hands, fingers interlocked and elbows tight. Once the guide finished, everyone finished. Usually, there wasn't a ton of chaos here; this happened outside the chow hall in the sandpit.

Our days consisted of a variety of trainings and courses, such as Marine Corps history, customs and courtesies, first aid, uniforms, leadership, close order drill, physical fitness, and swim qualification. Every day was jam-packed. If there happened to be a break between trainings, the drill instructors would take us to the pit and destroy us, make us clean our rifles over and over, or make us scrub the squad bay from top to bottom. At times, they would wreak havoc on the squad bay; other times, they would play cruel games.

One evening in particular, we had just showered and were standing on line in front of our racks, waiting to be inspected by our drill instructor. We wore our tighty-whities with our skivvy shirts folded and tucked into the back of our underwear like tails. The DIs would inspect our shave, fingernails, and toenails and look for anything that appeared infected. Once the inspections were complete, each recruit was to have a full canteen to chug before we hit the rack. Forced hydration is a thing. Gripping the canteen tight with both hands, elbows parallel, we drank the entire canteen without stopping and were to hold it upside down over our head when finished. Occasionally, a recruit would try to beat the system and get caught. From the start, this recruit's canteen was empty, and the drill instructor noticed. I swear to you he was so angry that you would have thought flames were coming out of his ears. Not only did every one of us have to refill our canteens, but this recruit had to continue drinking until he finally puked it all up. Guess who had to clean up his vomit while he was forced to drink more. That's right: the recruits around him. I'm pretty sure that after that night, that recruit always had a full canteen—and everyone made sure he did.

At the end of every day, we had about one hour to ourselves before we hit the rack. This hour went by extremely fast though. During this time, we showered, shaved, took a poop (since we couldn't during the day), brushed our teeth (since we didn't have time in the morning), cleaned our boots, prepped our uniforms, studied for upcoming tests, wrote or read letters, organized our footlockers, and cleaned the head and shower room.

I'm thankful that each night before we hit the rack the drill instructors would let us gather in a prayer group. I looked forward to this every night; saying a prayer with my brothers put me at ease for the night. Recruit Timothy Creager led our prayers for our Christian group. The memories of his prayer group will stick with me forever, as his name is tattooed on my chest: Lance Corporal Timothy Creager. He was killed in action in Iraq on my twenty-first birthday, which was in 2004. I'll talk more about this in a later chapter.

Our first five weeks of training took place at MCRD San Diego, but weeks six through nine took place at Camp Pendleton—or as we called it, "up north." Up north is where our basic warrior training took place, including long, torturous hikes; the gas chamber (better known as the marine cry room); land navigation; combat and confidence courses; rifle qualification; and most important, the crucible.

The crucible is a test every recruit must pass to earn the title of US Marine. It will test not only your physical strength but your mental strength as well. Over fifty-four hours, we marched over forty-five miles. We had a total of three meals ready to eat (MREs), and we averaged about two hours of sleep per night. We completed team building and leadership activities, combat obstacle courses, and long hikes—all while severely sleep and energy deprived. The final stretch of the crucible was the final hike back to the barracks. We stepped off at 0230 for a 9.7-mile hike that included a seven-hundred-foot-tall mountain called the Reaper.

The day after the crucible was over, we were permitted to make a thirty-second phone call home. I was nine weeks into training, feeling a massive sense of accomplishment, and missing my family like crazy, and the only person I wanted to call was my mom. She had written me a letter every single day up to that point. As the phone was ringing, I prayed she would pick up. Sure enough, she picked up, and all of a sudden something came over me.

"Hello?" Mom said.

"Mom," I said as I struggled to get words out.

"Jared! Is that you?"

I lost it. I started crying hysterically. "Yes, it's me."

"Oh my. Are you okay?"

I struggled to catch my breath. "Yes."

"I miss you," she said.

"I … miss … you … too." I could not talk easily because of how emotional I became.

The drill instructor interrupted. "Hang up. Time is up."

"I … have … to … go."

"I miss you, and I love you. We will see you next month," Mom said. She was crying too.

I forced out a few more words. "I love you too."

Later that day, as I was feeling depressed and disappointed that I wasted my only call home and my talk with mom, the drill instructors got a wild idea to play games with us since we got to use the phone. It started with them storming out of their office and making up a story that we did something wrong. First, we had to dump our footlockers into the middle of the squad bay and make a "salad."

"Everybody outside *now!*" one of the kill hats screamed.

As we trampled our way down three flights of stairs and into formation, we were instructed to fill our pockets with dirt. "Get back upstairs right now!" he shouted.

Once we were back on line in front of our racks, looking at our "salad" we'd made, the next command was to make a sandstorm. All sixty of us grabbed handfuls of dirt from our pockets and threw it in the air. It wasn't over though. Next, the drill instructors told us to make it snow. So we each grabbed a bottle of foot powder and squeezed until the bottles were empty. To top it off, we had to make it rain. We tossed water from sixty canteens all over the dirt and foot powder. The rest of the night was a blast; the drill instructors disappeared into their office and told us that the squad bay had better be spotless when they returned. Hours later, we recovered all our respective gear and scrubbed the squad bay back to its original state.

The final three weeks of training after returning to MCRD were much more relaxed. I'm not sure if it was more comfortable or if we were just used to all the nonsense and knew how to deal with the drill instructors. In the final weeks, we would catch ourselves laughing more at them rather than being afraid. Our humor often backfired on us, and we suffered the consequences.

One day, we had just returned to the barracks from physical training and were sweaty and ready for a quick shower when someone set off a drill instructor. "Take your boots off right now!" the kill hat shouted. "Throw your boots into a pile right now," he said as we all hurried to the center of the squad bay and made an enormous mound of dirty tan boots. The DI began grabbing boots and tossing them in the air and mixing up the boots as much as he could. "You have five seconds to grab two boots and get back on line!" the DI screamed as we frantically rushed to grab two mismatched boots. "Tie those boots together and get into the rain room now!"

Once all sixty recruits trampled one another and made our way into the shower, we were instructed to turn the shower heads on and get back on line. After the DI was finished playing games with us, we had the pleasure of digging through 120 soaking wet boots to find our personal pair, which was marked with our number underneath the tongue.

Graduation day finally came. Up until this point in my life, not only were these the hardest days, but they were also the most rewarding; the sense of pride and accomplishment was over the top. I still get goosebumps thinking about walking across the parade deck, marching in perfect formation as hundreds of family members and friends cheered for us. When my senior drill instructor handed me my Eagle, Globe, and Anchor and said, "Congratulations, Marine," my life changed forever. I had earned the title that few others have or could. I had become part of the most feared fighting force in the world and now belonged to something bigger than myself.

After graduation, I headed home for a brief ten-day leave, and then I was headed right back to Camp Pendleton, California, to report to the School of Infantry, an eight-week course designed to teach us infantry marines more advanced combat and weaponry skills. It consisted of eight weeks of sleeping in the field; patrolling; mastering our AR-15s, machine guns, grenades, rockets, and grenade launchers; learning land navigation; and much more. During infantry school, there was a sign-up sheet to become a light armored vehicle (LAV) crewman. LAV crewmen are still infantry but hold two infantry billets: 0311 rifleman and 0313 LAV crewman. Quite a few of us volunteered for LAV school upon graduation from infantry school. LAV school was six weeks long and just across the street from the school of infantry, so we didn't have to go far. As LAV crewman and active duty marines, we could be attached to one of three units: First, Second, or Third Light Armored Reconnaissance Battalion (LAR). First LAR was at Camp Pendleton; Second LAR was at Camp Lejeune, North Carolina; and Third was at Twenty-Nine Palms, California. Our whole graduating class was sent to Camp Lejeune and split up between Alpha, Bravo, Charlie, Delta, and Headquarters companies. We arrived in December 2003.

Welcome to the Fleet Marine Force!

CHAPTER
THREE

Ride a Bull, City Boy

Upon arriving at our assigned company, we were informed we were leaving in just a few weeks to head out to Twenty-Nine Palms, California, for two months of desert warfare training because we would be deploying to Iraq in September 2004. This training helped us prepare for our upcoming combat deployment; we lived in tents when we weren't in the field, it rained a lot, and nights were freezing. When we returned home, the training didn't stop. Week after week, month after month, we prepared for Fallujah, knowing what was coming down the pipe. Delta Company was the first to deploy in March.

We were down to three months until we were scheduled to deploy and replace Delta Company in September. I had just returned to base after celebrating my twenty-first birthday in Florida. Shortly after arriving back at Camp Lejeune, a few of us marines were hearing rumors that someone in Delta Company had been killed in action. Once the next of kin was notified, we were given the official word that Lance Corporal

Timothy Creager had been killed in action on July 1, 2004. I was devastated. After hearing the news, I wept for hours in my barracks room. Creager and I both had the same billet; we were drivers.

Hearing of his death infuriated me but also terrified me. I thought of the memories we had had together for the past fourteen months; we had become brothers. Not only had we been in the same platoon in boot camp, but he had also led our nightly prayer group before hitting the rack. He had been a model recruit, both physically and mentally. After graduation, we had attended the School of Infantry for eight weeks, followed by six weeks of LAV School. Our weekends were fun filled off base, and he had never let us get into trouble. Creager was not only a model marine but a model Christian as well. We were assigned to Second LAR Battalion in Camp Lejeune, North Carolina. I went to Alpha Company, and Creager to Delta.

Delta Company deployed to Iraq first and crossed the line of departure (LOD) into Iraq on March 4, 2004. They saw consistent combat throughout the early months in and around the Fallujah area. On July 1, their platoon was on a routine vehicle patrol down one of the main routes just outside Fallujah. A company of LAVs consisted of four LAV-25s. A LAV looks like a tank with eight wheels, and the number 25 represents the main gun, which is a 25 mm Bushmaster chain gun. And yes, it's a beast. Each vehicle has a driver, a gunner and a vehicle commander up in the turret, and four scouts in the back. The scouts are marines who can quickly dismount and maneuver on foot wherever they are needed.

That day, Lance Corporal Creager's vehicle had a different vehicle commander. Their original vehicle commander, the marine who had trained with the crew leading up to the deployment, had been shot a few days earlier. Their LAV was the rear vehicle in the patrol, and they were traveling about thirty miles per hour. The road was a three-lane paved highway with guardrails lining the left side. Just like in the States, there was a dirt median in between guardrails on both the northbound and southbound lanes. Corporal Simms and Lance Corporal Creager were great friends. During the patrol, they were having a conversation over the intercom system; they were, of course, talking about back home. Creager said to Simms, "When we get home, I'm going to take your city butt to the country and teach you how to ride a bull." Just then, Corporal Simms saw a bright flash to the front left of the vehicle and was knocked unconscious from a massive blast. Their vehicle was struck by an improved explosive device (IED) that was hidden behind the guardrail.

When Corporal Simms became conscious, he was hanging over the left side of the turret and realized the vehicle was engulfed in flames. He tried to scramble out, but something kept pulling him back into the vehicle. He'd try again, but again he would be pulled back into the turret. Finally, he cleared his head enough to notice the wire that was connected from his helmet to the radio was not disconnecting. After pulling off his helmet, Corporal Simms quickly jumped over the back of the turret and screamed for help. The marines and corpsman were able to pull him to safety, but not before he suffered third-degree burns to his face and hands and took three gunshot wounds to the leg.

The vehicle burned to rubble, the scouts walked away with minor injuries, the vehicle commander was severely wounded, and Lance Corporal Creager was killed instantly from the blast. Corporal Simms spent months in the hospital while undergoing skin grafts and numerous other surgeries before he left the marines in 2008. These marines and those in the platoon who responded to the attack are real heroes.

Over the next three months, as we prepared to deploy, my mind was all over the place. I couldn't wait to get over there and get revenge; at the same time, I was terrified of the unknown. A week before I deployed, I created a handwritten will for my family. I was mentally preparing myself for death. We knew we were going to Fallujah, and we knew what we were going to face. I made my mother promise that no matter what, she would follow the will if something happened to me. I reminded her that no news was good news and not to worry.

Easier said than done.

On September 4, 2004, we departed Cherry Point, North Carolina, for our long flight to Kuwait, where our vehicles were waiting on us. When we stepped off the plane, it was just like the scene from the movie *Jarhead*, except we weren't in the comfort of a theater and the heat was real—146 degrees, to be exact.

Over the next week in Kuwait, we prepared for our move up to Iraq. We zeroed in our weapons, performed maintenance on our vehicles, and had lengthy briefs about our mission in Fallujah. Kuwait was hot when we were out in the field training in the days leading up to our departure; our water bottles were air temperature (140–150 degrees). To cool down our scalding-hot drinking water, we would shove the bottle in a wet sock and tie it to the side of the vehicle as we drove through the desert. The hot air hitting the damp sock cooled the water just a few degrees.

On September 10, 2004, we loaded our vehicles in preparation for our three-day road march to Fallujah. Typically, this drive would take around five hours; however, since we had an entire company of vehicles—approximately twenty—we prepared to take it slow.

Lance Corporal Timothy Creager doing what he loved.

FOUR

Operation Phantom Fury

Midnight. September 11, 2004. Locked and loaded, ready to cross the LOD from Kuwait into Iraq. One hundred thirty marines loaded into twenty vehicles and made their weapons condition one, meaning rounds in the chamber and ready to fire. As I sat in my driver's seat with the hatch closed tight, I glared through my periscopes at the point of entry into Iraq. I thought back on the newspaper article I read that motivated me to join the Corps. "Marines Invade Iraq." Over the past sixteen months, I had gone from stepping on the yellow footprints as a nasty civilian to a US Marine about to cross into Iraq on the third anniversary of the very day that had changed the future of our country. The emotions were high that night. We were well trained and had all the resources we needed to fight; however, Iraq was the unknown for the majority of us, and that created anxiety. "Lord, please watch over us, and bring us all home to our families," I prayed as the commanding officer (CO), Captain Griffin, came over the radio. He said, "Oscar Mike." ("On the move.")

As we stepped off, the diesel engines from our vehicles roared, and our exhaust filled the air. We were unstoppable: four 25 mm Bushmaster chain guns, antitank missiles, mortars, grenade launchers, rockets, AR-15s, machine guns, air support, and all the equipment needed to operate in complete darkness. LAVs are equipped with a periscope that interchanges with a digital heat sensor screen; we used this screen at night when driving blacked out. The picture on the screen provides only a thirty-degree field of view, the image is black-and-white and only two-dimensional, and operating the vehicle safely takes months of practice for not only the depth perception but for your eyes to adjust to the screen. Over the previous days, while training in Kuwait, I had been having a hard time driving with the screen because of extreme nausea. So we took a chance, and First Sergeant Link allowed me to keep the periscope in, for the roads were lined with streetlights the whole route. As I think back, this was a dumb mistake on my part. What if we had to go off road or the lights went out as they did multiple times every night in Iraq?

Crossing into Iraq put an unsettling feeling in our stomachs; at times, I was unsure if this was real or a dream. The night air was crisp, which was a refreshing feeling after days of 140-plus degrees in the scorching sun. I can still vividly remember the smell of the Iraqi air; it was a mixture of trash and manure. We drove north at what seemed to be parade speed, mile after mile, passing hole after hole in the road from previous IEDs. A typical passenger car traveling sixty miles per hour would make this particular route in five or six hours; it took our company nearly three days. Every hour, we stopped to inspect our vehicles. We ate on the move, peed in bottles, and were always at the ready for enemy contact. Just a few hours into our road march, a vehicle broke down, so we rigged for the tow and continued on our way. We saw firefights in the distance, but we never took contact. I wouldn't mess with us either.

Along the route, Corporal Early, our scout, would drive for an hour or two so I could rest and provide security. At various bases along the way, we stopped, performed maintenance, ate chow, and slept for an hour before we were right back on the road. At three in the morning, we finally arrived at our destination: Camp Baharia, a small camp parallel to Camp Fallujah. Before American troops occupied Camp Baharia, Dreamland had been the name. The property had been occupied by two of Saddam Hussein's sons, Uday and Qusay Hussein. According to rumors, Uday and Qusay would snatch up women from Fallujah, bring them to Dreamland, and have their way with them. After arriving, unpacking, and debriefing in total darkness, we grabbed cots to sleep on in a nearby tent, only to be woken up a few hours later by a rocket that hit just on the other side of the compound wall, about one hundred feet away.

Welcome to Fallujah!

Over the next week, Delta Company schooled us in the area. Their goal was to train us on the dos and don'ts of the area of operation (AO), how to stay alive, and what to look for. They had been beaten up pretty bad—not as bad as the enemy—and were ready to get back to the States.

Once Delta departed Fallujah, Alpha took over, and we began our preparation for the anticipated battle. Over the next month, we patrolled the outskirts of Fallujah. As we prepared for Operation Phantom Fury, our mission was to snatch up insurgents attempting to evade the city, and we allowed 90 percent of the city—mostly women and children—to depart. They knew what was coming, and so did we. Officials estimated four to five thousand insurgents were operating in the city, led by Abu Musab al-Zarqawi. We had some close calls with rockets and mortars during our patrols, as well as on base. Almost daily, we would take incoming of some sort, either rockets or mortars. Luckily, insurgents are poorly trained and not the brightest crayons in the box. They could never get one directly on us, except once. One afternoon, Lance Corporal Kylo and I were in the workout tent while lifting weights when a rocket came soaring in and landed next to the tent. It was a dud. The rocket was stuck in the dirt and didn't explode—yet another sign how God had decided it wasn't my time.

Around the first of November, two television reporters were assigned to our unit; specifically, they were assigned to ride on my vehicle. They were Elizabeth Palmer and J. R. Hall from CBS News. At the time, they were two who reported the majority of the news back to the States. We knew what was about to go down, even though us lower-level marines didn't have all the details yet. We finally received the green light. Our mission was to cordon off Fallujah, letting no one in or out. We filled our packs with as much as we could fit and strapped them to the outside of the vehicles; we were prepared to fight. Because the insurgents were trapped and were preparing to fight to the death within the city, day and night they attempted to drop mortars on us. Because of this, we frequently had to change our location; they continued to get closer and closer. One afternoon, we were tucked back on top of a hill with an excellent vantage point of the city when mortars started coming in. Each mortar continued to land closer; the enemy was learning how to adjust and walk-in each shot. We quickly loaded the vehicles and moved about two hundred meters away. Then, a mortar landed precisely where one of the LAVs had been parked just moments earlier. It had been a great call by Captain Griffin, our CO.

The weather began to change around this time of year. Not only were the days getting cooler and the nights getting cold, but the rain had started to fall. Rain made it difficult to perform our duties at night because of our thermal sensors and night vision goggles (NVGs) kept washing out. We couldn't see anything. We were soaking wet and freezing with nowhere to dry off in the hostile enemy territory. Sleeping was nearly impossible; the rain had soaked through our water-resistant sleeping bags and saturated our already wet clothes, with temperatures getting down into the fifties at night.

On November 6, with the city completely cordoned off, all troops moved into position in preparation for the attack. Regimental Combat Team One and Regimental Combat Team Seven, along with two thousand Iraqi soldiers, waited patiently on the northern outskirts, ready to dance with the supposed four thousand insurgents. Earlier that day, our company had been attacked two separate times. The first was Lieutenant Pharis's crew; they had been on a routine vehicle patrol when a suicide bomber in a car sped toward them and exploded. The car was in pieces, the engine block was a hundred meters away, shrapnel was everywhere, body parts were spread over the road, and a massive crater marked where the car had detonated. Luckily, Lieutenant Pharis was the only marine wounded, and his injuries weren't life threatening. The second attack had happened shortly after that when a buried IED detonated next to Sergeant Palacio's vehicle. He was injured as well, but thankfully his injuries were not serious.

Our company was part of Regimental Combat Team One,

and our mission was to guard the southern border of Fallujah. We were to engage combatants as they were forced to the south by the US troops approaching from the north.

Combat started almost immediately; we were attacked by mortars, rockets, and small arms fire. We returned fire with our 25 mm Bushmaster chain guns, M240 machine guns, mortars, antitank missiles, and rifles. We also coordinated with Cobra helicopters; they would fly overhead and fire missiles to light up the insurgents. Artillery stayed busy twenty-four hours a day. A few times every hour, artillery rounds flew over our heads and demolished buildings filled with insurgents. At night, they would fire white phosphorus shells. These rounds would explode a few hundred feet above the ground and rain down on the enemy, creating havoc.

On November 12, yet another one of our vehicles was struck by an IED, this time in the small hostile town of Karma just outside Fallujah. Two marines were wounded, Votrobek and Laracuente. Vot, as we called him, was a close friend of mine. Their objective was a humanitarian effort; they were handing out food to the local children. The four LAVs were set up in a field in the center of town, and their vehicles were about two hundred meters apart, facing outward in a coil formation. The marines were in the center of the coil, talking to the children, when a mortar landed in the coil, followed by three more. The kids scattered as the marines quickly loaded the vehicles to evade the area. As they sped up the main road, Vot noticed the women and children outside taking shelter. Everyone felt the unnerving vibe; something was about to go down.

As the crew turned the corner, two IEDs exploded only four feet from Vot as their vehicle caught fire from the punctured can of diesel fuel strapped to the outside of the

LAV. His machine gun was blown out of his hands and landed in the basket on the rear of the turret. Vot was temporarily blinded from the blast as he took shrapnel to the face and arms. The next thing he heard was the M240 machine gun firing from the turret. He was helpless; all he could do was wait for help. Next, the gunner pulled Vot and Laracuente out of the back hatch and ran them to safety.

Simultaneously on the other side of town, my crew was sitting at Forward Operating Base (FOB) Karma when we heard, felt, and saw the blast. We were already loaded up and ready to go because of the previous mortar attack. Usually, we would receive word to stand down if there were no casualties or if the vehicles were not damaged. This time, we knew it was different. Four mortars followed by two IED blasts and then machine gun fire meant it was go time.

We started to head in their direction; we were only about a quarter mile down the road. Over the radio, I heard, "Two wounded marines, Votrobek and Laracuente." I was already driving as if I were at the Indy 500, but when I heard the name of my friend, my anxiety soared.

As we arrived at the medevac location, Doc treated the casualties, loaded them up on the stretchers, and put them in my vehicle, and then we were off. I drove that vehicle as fast as I could safely drive, trying not to get blown up on the way to the hospital. I drove as if I were transporting expensive china in the back. We arrived at Camp Fallujah safely and were able to get these marines the care they needed. Vot was later sent home because of hearing damage.

Occasionally, incidents happened that initially seemed negligent and put our safety in jeopardy. Later, however, we would laugh uncontrollably, especially if it was the company first sergeant who messed up. One evening as we posted outside Fallujah on a screen line, we were all mounted on our vehicles, providing overwatch. At night, especially in a combat zone, it was vital to remain blacked out so we weren't easy targets. It was no secret we were there; our fourteen-ton LAVs and rumbling engines gave us away. The time was midnight, the moonlight was dim, the crickets were loud, and there was sporadic gunfire in the distance. In an instant, a white flare shot fifty feet above my vehicle and lit up our entire area where our vehicles were located like a spotlight shining down on us. It took about thirty seconds for the flare to burn out and hit the ground. Right away, the CO came over the radio, asking who shot the flare. No one could figure out why or how someone would pop a flare for no reason. First Sergeant Link came over the radio and said, "Sorry about that, Marines. That was my mistake. I had the flare sitting on top of the turret, and I accidentally knocked it down, the primer hit, and it shot straight up between my legs and into the sky. Disregard, and carry on." After the panic and anxiety went away, we all had a pretty good laugh.

On November 13, another IED attack occurred, but this time there were no casualties. We also had a few small arms attacks that day. On November 16, four marines were wounded by a rocket attack, with no life-threatening injuries. November 16 marked the day that Fallujah was determined to be all clear. There were still periodic attacks and firefights happening; however, the battle was over. During the ten-day siege, approximately fifty-one US troops lost their lives, and 425 were wounded. Eight Iraqi soldiers were killed, with approximately forty-three wounded. Perhaps close to fifteen hundred insurgents were killed; the rest fled the city.

On November 18, we were called to medevac a soldier from another unit; he was an army sergeant who had been hit by an IED. When we arrived at his location, he had already lost a lot of blood. Doc Gartmann and Lance Corporal Early treated Sergeant Nolan and kept him alive until we arrived at the hospital in Camp Fallujah. Later that day, Sergeant Nolan died from his wounds.

In the following days, our company received orders that we would be moving into the city and taking control of four abandoned Iraqi houses on the northern peninsula. Our mission was to provide a constant presence and overwatch to deter insurgent activity. Over the next few months, our company suffered two more IED attacks that wounded more marines. During our time on the peninsula, we controlled the point of entry into the city and screened all people for the first Iraqi election on January 30, 2005. Our primary purpose was to ensure insurgents were not able to get into the city as suicide bombers, and we were successful.

In February 2005, we departed the city of Fallujah and moved back to Camp Baharia. Our primary focus for the rest of the deployment, until April, was to patrol the outskirts of the city and conduct counterinsurgency missions. After an entire seven months in Iraq, Alpha Company was able to go home without a single marine killed. It was indeed a blessing from God mixed in with our outstanding marines and chain of command.

Until next time, Iraq!

The crew of Black 8 at the entry to Camp
Fallujah, Iraq, on November 4, 2004.

FIVE

Welcome Back

September 9, 2006, came all too quickly. It seemed as if we had just returned home from our last deployment, and here we were, headed back to the sandbox. This time though, my rank and billet changed; I was promoted to corporal and earned my way into the vehicle commander (VC) role. Not only was I the VC, but I was also the lead vehicle of our platoon and, at times, the company and battalion. During our trip from North Carolina to Kuwait, I had a lot running through my mind. *Am I trained well enough to perform my duties as a VC? Will we come home alive? The lives of my crew of seven are in my hands; can I handle this? Either way, we were all warriors.* I did not doubt that everyone was mentally and physically prepared to go to war.

After a long flight from Cherry Point, North Carolina, to Canada and on to Germany, we finally landed in Kuwait. Same as last time, we were blasted in the face with the heat as we stepped off the plane; this time, it was only 126 degrees. We headed to Camp Virginia, where we would prepare for our flight on a C-130 into Al Asad Air Base in Iraq. By chance, we crossed the LOD into Iraq on September 11—the same date as we had in 2004. Over the following few days, we prepared for our road march to Rawah. We zeroed in our weapons, performed vehicle maintenance, and sat in debrief after debrief. Gunny Yoshida, the company ops chief, was in the advanced party and had arrived in the country three weeks earlier. He told us how much better the enemy was this time around and that we had better have our heads on straight. I spoke to a marine from Third LAR, and he told us how dangerous the IEDs were and how his entire crew had been killed. As the departure date came closer, my fear of the unknown worsened, and my conversations with God became more frequent. The next morning, I was called into a briefing with the lieutenants and learned I was the point vehicle for the entire battalion for the trip up to Rawah.

Talk about pressure. I was twenty-two years old, it was my first time in Iraq as a VC, and I was assigned to lead an entire battalion through an IED-infested AO. The best part was that I didn't have a map. Our maps hadn't arrived yet, and all I had was a GPS. It wasn't like a GPS of today; rather, it consisted of numbers and an arrow, no roads, and no Siri. But the two-and-a-half-hour drive was a success. I didn't get us lost, and we didn't get hit by an IED. As we entered the town, Delta Company was headed out. The locals were yelling at them and throwing rocks at their vehicles as they drove down the street. Finally, we arrived at Combat Outpost (COP) Rawah, but we didn't stay long.

The next evening, at around 2200, we loaded up our vehicles and headed out. Our mission was to drive out to the traffic control point (TCP) and provide security for the evening. As we left the wire for the first time blacked out at night, I was a nervous wreck. The moon wasn't out, there were no streetlights on because all the power in the town was out, and I was using NVGs to navigate an area that was utterly foreign to me. Not only that, but I was the lead vehicle and my crew and platoon were relying on me. When we finally made it to TCP-5, each vehicle oriented in a different direction. Two of us had a desert view, and the other two LAVs had vantage points down the main supply route (MSR). For the remainder of the night, until the sun came up, we rotated for fire watch, and we switched every two hours.

The next morning, the lieutenant informed us that our platoon would be taking control over TCP-5 and making it home until further notice. We weren't too thrilled. TCP-5 didn't look too exciting when the sun came up. It consisted of a three-way intersection, a north and south route for MSR Bronze, and the only road into Rawah. About one hundred yards to the west, on top of a hill, sat our shelter, our home for the next two months. This shelter was not built to withstand weather; it was made to protect us from incoming mortars and rockets. Whereas the walls were six-foot-thick, ten-foot-tall barriers filled with dirt, our overhead "protection" for the ten-by-fifteen area consisted of plywood and one layer of sandbags. The ground was what we liked to call "moon dust," and we were lucky to have cots to sleep on. Our bathroom was about fifty feet from the shelter and consisted of a lawn chair with a hole cut out and a toilet seat screwed on. We dropped a bag into the toilet seat, did our business, and then disposed of the bag into the burn pit. There wasn't a shower, so that was out of the question. TCP-5 was pretty much paradise.

About one hundred yards south was a post for Iraqi soldiers. Their job was to assist us on the TCP by translating as well as searching people and vehicles under our supervision.

The Iraqi soldiers weren't the brightest bunch; I often thought they had the IQ of a hamster.

A few days into our stay at paradise, I was attempting to take a nap after a long patrol. I was lying on my cot, with headphones in my ears and my CD player on my chest. After dozing off for a few minutes, an enormous explosion jolted me awake. I was utterly stunned and panic stricken. When I was able to focus, I quickly put my gear on. We learned God was on our side for this attack; a mortar round had landed within ten feet of our shelter, just on the other side of the wall from where I had been sleeping. If the round had traveled ten more feet, it would have landed directly in our hooch and killed us all.

For the next couple of months, we continued to control the TCP and patrol the MSR and all other roads, as well as the desert in our AO. Counterinsurgency was our focus. We had some close calls—IEDs that we found before detonation, weapon caches, and of course the incoming mortar attacks that happened every few days. Often we would drop marines in the desert in the middle of the night to provide reconnaissance and attempt to catch the insurgents shooting mortars; however, each time our attempts were unsuccessful.

Around the end of October, the weather started to change. The hot temperatures began to subside, and the rainy season was underway. Living outside without shelter in a cold and rainy environment made us rethink our decision to be marines. On the night of October 28, we endured a horrible thunder-and-lightning storm, which was a bit unnerving because all seven of us wet and smelling marines were crammed into one metal vehicle to try to sleep. The next morning, as I was sitting in the turret on fire-watch duty and listening to radio transmissions, I heard a loud blast and spotted a mushroom cloud in the distance. As I sat there waiting, I prayed it wasn't our marines who were hit. Radio silence broke, and the news came through. First Platoon suffered devastating injuries while patrolling through town. They were on a routine foot patrol through a dried-up creek bed when two buried IEDs exploded at the same time under their feet. Almost every marine on patrol was wounded—some more than others. The marine who took the worst of the blast was Lieutenant Kinard, who had been standing directly on top of one of the buried IEDs when an insurgent remotely detonated it. He was thrown thirty feet in the air but luckily was still alive, yet he was losing blood fast. Not only were the other marines and corpsmen wounded, but they also had no choice but to direct everyone else to provide security, call in a quick reaction force (QRF), and treat the wounded. These marines and corpsmen are heroes. Once QRF arrived thirty-five minutes later, the casualties were evacuated by helicopter to Al Asad Air Base. Lieutenant Kinard and the other wounded marines survived. Lieutenant Kinard ended up losing both of his legs and endured numerous other surgeries over the next few years.

Little did we know that this attack was the first of many to come.

The crew of White 2 just outside of Anah, Iraq, in 2006.

SIX

Ready to Fight

The paradise of TCP-5 came to an end. Our new mission was to take over the AO for Second Battalion, Eighth Marines, which was the small but densely populated town of Anah. It was saturated with insurgents. No longer would we be conducting vehicle patrols, for the streets were too narrow and dangerous to maneuver. We would be sitting ducks for IED and RPG attacks. But we were most excited about our new COP. No longer would we stay in a dirt hooch; our new home was COP Ocatal, which had been a youth center similar to a YMCA. The building was located in the dead center of town and surrounded by a mosque, a town hall, a half-constructed building, a soccer field, and residential neighborhoods. The compound had a ten-foot-tall concrete wall surrounding most of the property, and we had concertina wire surrounding it, about one hundred yards out. There were two points of entry into our COP. The front gate was constantly guarded by two marines, dirt barriers, and concertina wire. The back gate was for foot patrols to leave the compound. It was not defended, but the towers on the roof gave us the vantage point to provide overwatch for our whole compound. At least two marines were in each tower at all times, and a corporal of the guard was roving around.

Restricting access into Anah was a priority because counterinsurgency was our goal. We blocked off every vehicle entry point into the town except the main road, which was controlled by our marines at a TCP. To ensure unauthorized vehicles couldn't get into Anah, the engineers used bulldozers to build a six-foot-tall dirt berm around the perimeter. This was helpful, but it didn't stop motorcycles or pedestrians. During the early days of building the berm, we provided security for the engineering team and covered their backs while they worked. To adequately provide overwatch, we posted on top of a hill to ensure we had a solid vantage point; however, this put us at risk for sniper fire. During their operations, the engineers were lucky and ran over only two pressure plate IEDs that detonated. But because of the steel on the heavy equipment, no one was injured.

Overwatch was a tedious duty for us; as marines, we wanted action. The day went by, nightfall came around, and we were still posted on top of the hill providing overwatch when we heard a massive explosion in the city. Lieutenant Taylor told us to stand to and get ready to go, for we were the designated QRF. Lance Corporal Curry and Corporal Mann were not on the vehicle; they had just walked over to another vehicle to grab some MREs. Our sleeping gear was already laid out on the ground because we were prepared to stay overnight again. But then a Humvee was hit by an RPG and needed our support.

I was already mounted up and ready to go. Curry and Mann were still walking back, so I yelled at them to hurry up;

there was contact in the city. They laughed at me, thinking it was a joke, probably because our deployment up to this point had been slow. I then screamed at them. "Hurry up!" They got the message.

Once we were all mounted, we took off down the hill. As Curry was driving like a madman through rough terrain, I was trying to input the ten-digit grid of the attack into the GPS. I didn't have time to look at the map; it wouldn't have helped if I did though, because it was dark. As we hit the bottom of the hill, Curry ran us right through a ditch, which nearly tossed us out of the turret. We were the point vehicle, locked and loaded and ready to fight. Our adrenaline was pumping, and we had tunnel vision.

We entered the city through the TCP. I knew which general direction to go because of the arrow on the GPS; however, this was my first time driving through the city at night, and I was unfamiliar with the streets.

As soon as we pulled on to the first narrow street, my stomach dropped. It felt like a scene from the movie *Black Hawk Down* or—worse yet—a nightmare. There were houses on both sides of the street, only about ten feet from each side, and people were standing on the sidewalks while glaring at us. The lights were flickering on and off in the background when the city suddenly went pitch black. All the lights turned off at the same time, which was a common occurrence in Iraq. We were certain contact was coming.

As we approached the site of the RPG attack, the Humvee was engulfed in flames, and the fifty-caliber ammo was cooking off and firing rounds in random directions. We were low in the turret, locked and loaded. As the Humvee burned, we provided security while the corpsmen treated the casualty. He was a civilian contractor with lacerations to the kidney and multiple shrapnel wounds. As we scanned the area, preparing for an ambush, not a single round was fired at us. Our LAVs were intimidating, so no wonder insurgents didn't want to mess with us at close quarters.

We finally loaded up the wounded contractor and his crew, and I led the convoy out of the city and to the landing zone (LZ) to medevac the wounded. To ensure the burning Humvee wasn't booby-trapped, we left a squad of marines behind to provide security. Once the casualties were safely on the bird, we headed back to Anah to recover the Humvee. As we cordoned off the vehicle, it was still on fire and occasionally popping off ammo. After using a couple of fire extinguishers, we rigged the scorched Humvee and prepared to tow it out of town. The tires were melted, and the entire vehicle burned to just a metal frame. The only thing to survive was a half of a gas mask. I led the way as always; we dragged the hot scrap metal down the road until we were just outside town. We finally unhooked the torched Humvee and let it finish burning for the remainder of the night as we provided overwatch from the first hill we posted on. I'm not sure anyone slept because of the adrenaline pumping through our veins.

The next morning, we escorted a psychological operations (PSYOP) team through Anah to send a message about the previous night's RPG attack. As we rolled through town in our LAVs, we were surrounded by hundreds of people in the streets giving us the evil eye. Over the loudspeakers, PSYOP told them over and over in Arabic that the RPG attack did not affect us and that we were there to stay until all the insurgents were dead.

We were lucky enough to make a trip to COP Rawah after the PSYOP mission. Going back to COP Rawah was always exciting for us; it meant hot chow, maybe a shower, and a phone call home. However, during this month, it seemed that every time we came back, the phone center was shut down. Every time a service member was killed, all communications back to the States were cut off until the next of kin was notified. During the month of Ramadan, seventy-four marines and soldiers were killed, two from our battalion. We had no idea what November and December would bring as we began our foot patrols in Anah.

Once we ultimately moved into COP Anah, we were on the move day and night. A typical day for our squad was twenty or more working hours every day of the week. Since we had to have multiple guards and continuous patrols in the city, we operated twenty-four seven. Our rotation schedule was eight hours conducting foot patrols followed by eight hours standing guard either at the front gate or in one of the towers. The last eight hours consisted of numerous duties: we debriefed and briefed past and upcoming patrols, cleaned around the COP, cleaned our bodies, and when all was finished, slept for a few hours.

Our foot patrols started off right away with an IED attack. On November 11, our squad was on patrol searching random houses in Kilo sector when an IED exploded two streets over in Lima sector. Right away, I heard Third Platoon over the radio requesting QRF and saw them simultaneously shoot a red flare high in the air so that headquarters could identify their location. The IED had been hidden behind a sign and exploded as the patrol walked by. We stood fast, ready to support them, on guard and ready to take contact ourselves. We remained in position until QRF arrived and evacuated the two wounded marines. Both were knocked unconscious and took shrapnel to the legs, arms, and face.

During the months of November and December, our company took contact in some form or fashion almost daily. Enemy contact came in the form of sniper fire, hand grenades, RPGs, small arms fire, and IEDs, large and small. Luckily, the mortars finally stopped because we were in such a tight urban area. It was imperative that we had full gear on anytime we stepped outside, especially when climbing to the roof.

On November 18 at around 1500, it was my turn in the rotation for guard duty in the headquarters tower. As I climbed the ladder and began walking the twenty feet to the tower, it sounded like someone had set off a strip of Black Cat firecrackers at my feet. In an instant, I realized I was under machine gun fire from my right side, so I dropped to my stomach and placed my face on the gravel that lined the rooftop. The perimeter of the roof was lined with sandbags about two feet high. Rounds were penetrating them and ricocheting just over my head. After about ten seconds of continuous fire, I low crawled to the corner of the building, popped up, and scanned rapidly. On a berm about 150 yards away was a man dressed as a woman, and he held a machine gun. As soon as I returned fire, he dropped behind the berm and disappeared. This experience gave me what is known as the pucker factor.

As the days dragged on and we patrolled every day in a defensive state, our attitudes soured. Because of our rules of engagement (ROE) and a CO with minimal combat experience, we couldn't act until all levels of the ROE were met. Between mid-November and the end of December, over one-third of our company was wounded (approximately forty marines). We had so many marines getting sent home that combat replacements were sent in to join us; these were brand-new marines straight out of infantry school. During our patrols, we had the authority to enter any house or building we felt necessary, except the mosques. Intelligence and common sense told us this was where the insurgents were hiding and stockpiling weapons and explosives. Almost every time we were attacked, there was a mosque nearby, and soon after, an Iraqi would come over the loudspeaker and pray.

November 25 was an average day in Anah. Our squad had just finished eight hours of guard duty and begun a routine foot patrol. Our mission was to search multiple suspected houses that might be hiding a young man who had recently detonated an IED against one of our other squads. We were about three houses into our search when we headed up the main road north to the next block. Our squad was in a staggered formation, with a point man on the front right, followed by a marine on the left side of the road approximately twenty feet away. The remaining five marines and one corpsman were staggered the same. I was the fifth marine from the front walking on the right side of the road. As we approached the mosque about ten yards in front of me, a huge black cloud of smoke appeared.

The next thing I remember is waking up about ten seconds later, confused and disoriented. I immediately screamed for Lance Corporal Curry, who was carrying our radio. The smoke was still thick, and I couldn't see my hand in front of my face. My ears were ringing, so I couldn't hear if he was yelling back. Seconds later, I found Curry and instructed him to call for QRF. I simultaneously popped a red flare into the sky to signal the guard towers of our position and to let them know we were in distress. The IED blast had been so powerful that the concussion shut off my GPS. Once the GPS was able to reboot, which seemed like an eternity, we called in our exact location to headquarters.

As we were coordinating with QRF and giving them information about our location, we also informed them of how many casualties and who was wounded. Two marines were critically injured: Lance Corporal Herron and Corporal Aguirre, my gunner. A few other marines were wounded but were still able to roll over and provide security with their rifles. As we treated the casualties and provided security, we were cussing and screaming at the bystanders; we threatened to kill them if they came near us. Herron had been standing no more than three feet from the bomb when it exploded; once all was said and done, we had multiple tourniquets on him to help stop the bleeding. Aguirre was severely hurt as well; he had ended up running after he was hit and fell into a bush about thirty feet away.

Once QRF arrived, we loaded up the casualties. They all wouldn't fit on one LAV, so we had to spread them throughout the other vehicles. Herron was placed on a stretcher and put in the logistics LAV. I threw Aguirre over my shoulder and carried him to the other vehicle, bumping his head on the door as I put him in. We later had a good laugh about this. Once everyone was loaded and accounted for, I surveyed the area to ensure we did not leave behind any serialized gear that might end up in the hands of our enemy.

About eight minutes later, we arrived at the LZ and loaded the wounded marines on the helicopter. We told them we loved them and would take care of business while they were gone. Half of our squad was sent home that night, whereas the rest of us who were lucky enough to avoid the shrapnel wounds walked away with grade-three concussions and hearing loss.

After arriving back at COP Anah, the corpsmen evaluated and looked over us. They determined that my blurred vision, confusion, and hearing loss were due to a grade-three concussion. Because of that, I would have to remain on the COP for the next thirty days. Instead of patrolling, I assumed the role of corporal of the guard and oversaw the guard schedule.

IEDs and firefights continued over the next month; it was apparent everyone was distraught and fed up with the war.

The day before I was due to rejoin my squad and begin full duty again was December 24, Christmas Eve. I was standing guard in the tower on the headquarters building with Lance Corporal Orfitelli. The day was cold, and the sun was peeking around the clouds. I was observing the area around the mosque, about seventy-five yards away, while Orfitelli kept an eye on the rear of the building. As I stood there, helmet strap hanging down because I had grown complacent in the tower, my eyes were drawn to the sudden blast just in front of the entrance to the mosque. Instantly, I knew what this black smoke trail was: an RPG flying straight toward me. The tower was constructed out of plywood, and two layers of sandbags were stacked about chest high outside of the wood. Above chest high, we didn't have any protection, and this RPG was flying at my head. I froze like a deer in the headlights. My mind was telling me to take cover, but my body felt paralyzed. I couldn't react. Just as the RPG was about to fly into the tower and kill both Orfitelli and me, it curved downward and struck the roof air-conditioning unit about five feet away.

After the RPG exploded and sent a shock wave through our bodies, I finally fell to the ground. As my helmet fell off my head, we began to take small arms fire from an AK-47 coming from the same direction as the RPG blast. The rounds were flying into the tower and had us pinned down.

As I regained my composure, my hearing was gone, but I

knew I had to return fire. As the rounds continued to fly into the tower just inches over our heads, I reached up, cocked the M240 machine gun, took a deep breath, popped up, and started to return fire on full auto. I was able to suppress the enemy fire until the remaining marines were able to get into position around the perimeter of the building and return fire as well. In the end, we used a grenade launcher to blow up a fleeing car and put about three thousand rounds downrange in a matter of two or three minutes. Personally, I emptied two drums of the machine gun, approximately four hundred rounds, and emptied four magazines of my rifle, nearly 120 rounds.

After this day, we never had another attack against our compound.

CHAPTER

SEVEN

Merry Christmas

Christmas Day 2006 was not the Christmas happening back in the States. The snow wasn't falling, we weren't jolly, and Santa didn't visit. We did have a Charlie Brown Christmas tree though. A few days earlier, we had received intel that insurgents were going to attack us on Christmas Day. Because of this, our mission was to patrol the streets for the entire twenty-four-hour period. As we moved up and down each city block searching house by house, car by car, and nearly every military-age male we could find, we came up short.

About sixteen hours into our patrol, we posted on the roof of a building that had been a bank. The roof put us in a vulnerable position but gave us an excellent vantage point to provide overwatch. The roof was flat, with four-foot-tall concrete walls, and this offered us excellent cover. As we stood on the rooftop, looking out over the town toward an abandoned building, a bullet hissed past my head and hit the wall behind me. We went from boredom to firefight in a matter of two seconds.

As the rounds were hitting the wall behind us, we stood up and returned fire. As we fired our weapons, attempting to identify the suspect, a man walked out of an alley. He was walking briskly from our right field of view to the left about one hundred meters away. His trench coat was long and dirty; it was hard to tell if he was concealing a weapon. As we shouted at him in his native language to stop, he ignored our commands. After our fourth attempt to get him to stop, I gave the command to fire. The man's unresponsiveness to authority convinced me he was the shooter; we couldn't risk him getting away. We opened fire. He must have been on drugs because we hit him multiple times before he finally fell to the ground.

Minutes later, QRF arrived and confirmed the man was deceased. They loaded him into a body bag and brought him back to COP Anah. We knew the deceased man was an insurgent, so we tested his fingers for gunpowder residue, and he tested positive. He also had anti-American propaganda in his coat pocket. We determined he had been shooting at our squad and had ditched his weapon before walking out of the alley. Merry Christmas, marines!

Anah finally came to an end; we were mentally and physically exhausted. Thoughts of leaving for a patrol and dying were a constant state of mind for everyone. We were in desperate need of a change to regain our sanity.

In mid-January 2007, our next assignment was counterinsurgency in and around the town of Hasa, just north of Rawah. Our next COP was COP Hasa, which sat on a hilltop about a mile outside of town. Our perimeter was the size of about two football fields surrounded by concertina wire, and our shelter was fancy this time: tents with wooden floors. We had handmade wooden Porta Johns, and our urinals were buried PVC pipe sticking up about three feet above the ground at a forty-five-degree angle. As always, we didn't have a shower; we did, however, have electricity powered by generators. Best of all, we were out of Anah.

Over the next month, we were back doing vehicle patrols in and around Hasa. Day in and day out, we patrolled the area for suspicious cars, people, houses, and riverbanks and looked for weapons and possible IEDs. Because we were off road so frequently, our command decided it was a bright idea to attach a mine roller to the front of my vehicle and drive down dirt roads to clear them of any possible explosives. At this point in my deployment, the fear of death was no longer with me; if it was my time, it was my time. On top of that feeling, I didn't have a choice, so mine rolling it was. The mine roller was a solid-steel apparatus similar to a steamroller you'd see paving new roads. Mine was a bit smaller, with eight steel wheels lining the front, controlled by a remote control I held in the turret. With the remote, I could move the roller left or right as we drove, and it would allow me to push it farther than the wheels on my LAV. This nonsense continued off and on for a few weeks.

Because I am sitting here writing this book, you're probably guessing I didn't find an IED or land mine.

February 28, 2007, is another date tattooed on my chest. Our platoon returned to COP Hasa from an overnight mission along the Euphrates River. We had just wrapped up the debrief with the lieutenant when we heard a blast in the distance. Initially, we thought nothing of it because explosions were a dime a dozen in our area. However, over the next thirty minutes, it was evident something wasn't right.

48

Our command was acting odd, and nobody could tell us who got hit, so we continued to hang out in the tent. All I remember next is Sergeant Flood walking in and letting us know that Sergeant Allen's vehicle had been hit. Sergeant Flood had a blank stare, as if he had seen a ghost. A few of us shouted, "Are they okay? Was anyone hurt?"

He didn't answer and proceeded to look off into the distance with that blank stare.

I looked at him and asked, "Sergeant Flood, was someone killed?"

He still had a bewildered expression and no response.

"Who was it?" I asked. "Was it Sergeant Allen?"

He nodded.

The entire tent broke down. Every single marine was crying and in shock. Sergeant Flood walked over, sat next to me, and hugged me. I sobbed uncontrollably, with my face in his shoulder.

After we all gathered our composure, enough to keep a straight face, we were called to the headquarters tent for the official news. I kept replaying the last conversation I had had with Sergeant Allen. It had been the day before our squad left for our overnight patrol. We were talking about what we always talked about: working out and getting buff. He asked me what the best supplements were to gain muscle and lose fat.

I said, "As soon as we get back, let's go to the supplement store, and I'll get you set up."

He said, "Good to go. Have a safe patrol." Those were the last words I ever heard from him.

We all gathered around the entrance of the headquarters hooch as the company first sergeant informed us of what had happened. Just a few hours earlier, First Platoon had been patrolling a rural desert area out east, performing normal counterinsurgency operations. Sergeant Allen, as always, was leading the pack as the point vehicle for the patrol. The AO consisted of farmland, dirt roads, and a few houses lining the Euphrates River. Because Iraq doesn't benefit from massive amounts of rainfall, the Iraqi people pump water through metal pipes from the river to saturate the land. Our mission was never to destroy anything if we could avoid it; we always had the best interests of the people in mind. When patrolling, we avoided crossing choke points. These were areas that seemed like the only place to pass because of obstructions or obstacles in the terrain. Sergeant Allen and his team had a decision to make. As they approached the point where the water pipe ran under the road, they could have gone around the choke point and crushed the water pipe or crossed on the road where the pipe was buried. Because Allen was a kindhearted marine, he decided not to damage property and stay on the road to preserve the farmer's water pipe. As they cautiously approached, they scanned for wires, disturbed dirt, and trash that could be a potential IED, when suddenly their vehicle was hit by a massive pressure plate IED.

The bomb exploded under the front right of the LAV, which happened to be under the engine compartment. The blast tossed the fourteen-ton armored vehicle in the air like it was a toy, the front-right two tires were blown off, the engine compartment was gone, and the scouts in the back were thrown out. When the LAV finally hit the ground, it was engulfed in flames and lying on its left side. The marines in the other three vehicles provided security, checked for secondary IEDs, and immediately began pulling the wounded marines out and providing medical care as the platoon commander called in QRF. Sergeant Allen was killed on impact, for he was the vehicle commander and was up in the turret from his collarbone up. The gunner was down in the turret and suffered significant injuries, and the driver ended up getting his leg amputated.

When QRF finally arrived, the wounded marines were evacuated, and the burning vehicle was loaded up and hauled away. As we all stood listening to the First Sergeant tell the details of the fatal patrol, we mourned. It was only February 28; we still had another five weeks to go on the most arduous seven-month deployment of our lives. All we wanted was to go home and leave the evil country of Iraq.

The next day, our squad was right back on the road, except this time we all rode a little lower in the turret, and the complacency we used to have was long gone. We were laser focused, and deep down, we wanted revenge. Our mission was the same as always: counterinsurgency. As we approached the border of our AO, we decided to cut west across the desert. As I led the pack, I took a left off the MSR. My eyes were peeled for the safest place to cross the dried creek bed that separated the road from the desert—a spot we hadn't crossed before. We had been down this road hundreds of times and had passed in this area more times than I could count; it was crucial we didn't take the most accessible path. I crept forward. Our LAV dipped down through the untouched terrain.

Just as PFC Maher, my driver, started to accelerate, something came over me. I briefly saw a penny-size object in the dirt, looking like a piece of brown packing tape. As Maher pushed the gas and we started to move up through the back side of the creek bed, I screamed at the top of my lungs through the intercom. "Stop!" He slammed on his brakes, sending the crew flying forward in the turret. "Back up," I said.

As we moved back, I could see that our front tire tracks had stopped just inches from the small, seemingly inadequate object.

"What's the problem?" Lieutenant Taylor asked over the radio.

I responded, "I have a bad feeling about this small object in the dirt. I think we need to call EOD to come check it out. I think it's a possible pressure plate IED."

"Roger that," he said.

All four vehicles set up a coil, and we waited nearly two hours for the explosives crew to arrive. As they pulled up in their heavily armored vehicle, I directed them to the suspected IED, which I had marked with a water bottle. First, they sent the robot to investigate the area. The robot was equipped with cameras and multiple arms and levers to grab, pull, and dig. As it began digging the area around the suspected pressure plate, we could tell something was buried there. Twenty minutes later, the explosives team dismounted their vehicle and cautiously approached the site. They unveiled a two-foot-long pressure plate. It was two strips of metal wrapped in packing tape with a detonator in between the two pieces of metal, with a long wire coming out of the end and traveling into the ground. Shortly afterward, the crew dug up three oil jugs filled with forty-five pounds of rocket propellant. Digging up bombs was just another day in the office for the explosives team. They took the IED and destroyed it off-site. Here was just another example of our guardian angels at work; Sergeant Allen was watching over us. The volume of explosives that were packed into those bottles would have obliterated our LAV and killed all seven of us marines inside. Thank you, Sergeant Allen!

The next five weeks dragged on; day after day, we

conducted vehicle patrols in and around Hasa and the surrounding deserts. We searched car after car, man after man, and came up empty almost every time. The insurgents knew it was almost time to change battalions, so they sat back and waited. Why try to fight when there would be brand-new marines coming in and learning the area?

Finally, the first of April arrived. Many of us didn't think we would make it until the end, but we did.

Four weeks later, I completed my four years of military service and made the one-thousand-mile trip back to Missouri. Welcome home!

The pressure plate IED that we were inches
from driving over, ending our lives.

PART 2
Building the Legacy

You can't connect the dots looking forward; you can only connect them looking backwards. So you have to trust that the dots will somehow connect in your future. You have to trust in something—your gut, destiny, life, karma, whatever. This approach has never let me down, and it has made all the difference in my life.

—STEVE JOBS

EIGHT

Daddy's Little Girl

Four years as a US Marine finally came to an end. I planned to pursue my bachelor's degree at Lindenwood University in St. Charles, Missouri. Actually, this happened to be my only plan; I had no idea what I wanted to do after military service. Because fitness and nutrition were always passions of mine, I decided to make my way up to a local gym and apply to be a personal trainer.

Initially, I was turned down because it was considered the slow time of year in the fitness industry; I was told to come back in January. Of course, I didn't take no as an acceptable answer, so I applied to be a front-desk attendant and started working my first job post marines a few weeks later. Luckily, I was living with my brother at the time because minimum wage was not even making my car payment. I worked from 2:00 p.m. until the gym closed at 10:00 p.m. Every night, I'd meet up with friends at the bar and drink until early morning hours, sleep all day, wake up, and barely get to work on time the next afternoon. I was reckless and wild. Over the next two months, I repeated this cycle. I did, however, manage to make my way out to Lindenwood and enroll in the bachelor of arts in marketing program.

Over the next five weeks, I developed a relationship with the personal-training director at the gym, who happened to be a marine himself. He decided to give me a shot as a trainer and reminded me that June was not a great time to begin training. I ignored his caution and had every intention of proving him wrong. I had a strong desire and purpose to succeed as a trainer; I loved helping people and working out, and I was quickly running out of the money I had saved from my deployment.

Just as I planned, my first month started with a bang. I picked up eight new clients and was one of the top trainers in sales volume for the month of June. Yet even though personal training was going well, and I was scheduled to start school, I was on a downward spiral. The friends I chose to associate with wanted to drink at the bar every night, like me. I was spending every dollar I made, my anxiety was high, my temper was short, I was getting into fights, and I was on a path to self-destruction. To top it off, my brother was moving and I needed to find a new place to live. I didn't want to move back in with my mother and two younger brothers. I couldn't afford a place to live at the time, so I reached out to an old friend of mine I had reconnected with at the gym. John liked to party just as much as me; however, he had his head on straight and had a solid career as an accountant. I moved into his two-bedroom apartment a few days later.

Not a week later, I was in need of more clients on my schedule to ensure I could pay my rent every month. As I looked around the gym floor, I eyed a pretty woman who frequently attended my group-fitness classes. She was tall—about four inches taller than me—her long, blonde hair was pulled back in a ponytail, and she was wearing long basketball shorts and a T-shirt with cutoff sleeves. As she walked by me, I made eye contact, smiled, and started a conversation. I asked her if she ever had a trainer before and if she was interested in a complimentary workout. She agreed, and we set our appointment for the next day. At this point, I thought she was cute and had a great personality; however, it wasn't until I saw her in a short, black dress a few weeks later that I fell head over heels for her. We began spending time with each other more and more outside the gym. She was already in her career and had just finished her master's degree a few months back. I struggled to keep my confidence high around her; not only was she much taller than me, but she was more successful too. My income was barely paying the bills, I was struggling with anger and depression, I was a borderline alcoholic, and I had just begun working on my undergraduate degree. I felt inferior.

This young woman must have seen something in me that I didn't. Over the next couple of months, our feelings grew. We introduced each other to our families and friends and I began spending more time with her circle of friends than my friends. My attitude and focus slowly shifted from feeling down on myself to being excited about the future.

Nine months later, our future would forever change. Lyndsey was pregnant. Because we were both in love, we knew that everything would work out. Confused and scared of what the future held, we moved in together. I remember sitting in class one morning and thinking, *I better get my life together. I'm going to be a father.* At that moment, I made a decision. I decided wholeheartedly I was going to make a change and build a legacy for my future family. I had no idea how, but I was going to make it happen.

A month later, I heard that the gym was building a new location and was in need of a director of personal training. I knew this was my chance. My reputation was positive within the company, I was no longer drinking, I had a solid client base, and I was working on a business degree. After a few rounds of panel interviews, the owner of the company informed me they selected me for the position. My confidence skyrocketed; I had a sense of purpose and felt accomplished. Shortly afterward, I asked Lyndsey to marry me, and she said yes.

In June 2009, our daughter was born. A certain feeling came over me when I looked her in the eyes for the first time; it was not just unconditional love but a fire was lit inside my soul that has only burned hotter every day I see her. I had a desire to build a legacy for not only her but my fiancée and our future children too. I was officially a man on a mission.

Over the next nine years, I learned many hard lessons about life. I learned that my mind-set and actions controlled my future, so I ditched all excuses and took complete ownership of my life. In the remaining chapters, my goal is to help you learn and apply the habits and principles that helped me get to where I am today: a successful entrepreneur, businessman, father, and husband. If you can use these principles, your future is in your hands. You decide!

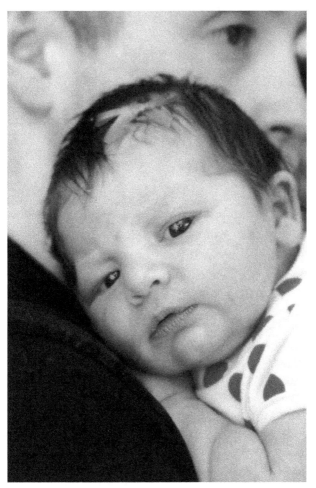

My oldest daughter when two days old.

CHAPTER

NINE

Breaking the Mold

When my oldest daughter was born, I had another decision to make: what would be the future of my family? You see, it was difficult for me to imagine anything more than living paycheck to paycheck, broke two days after payday, and using credit cards to pay off credit cards. When I was growing up, my family struggled. My parents worked hard to support my three brothers and me. They loved us unconditionally, but we knew from a young age they couldn't make ends meet. Their inability to provide a financially stable lifestyle wasn't due to a lack of ability, effort, or knowledge; rather, they didn't know any better due to their upbringing. I knew that if things were going to change, I had to change. Breaking the mold from a poverty mind-set is a difficult task, but I was tired of being broke and in debt, and I was disgusted with myself. I started out by asking myself two questions.

- What do I currently have in my life that I don't want?
- What do I currently want that I don't have?

Some of the things I had on my list of "things I don't want" were debt, negative people, and my anxiety and short temper. On my "things I want" list, I had financial freedom, debt freedom, a dream home, a successful career, positive friends, successful mentors, and many more. My lists got me excited, even though reaching these goals seemed nearly impossible because of where I came from.

Once I was clear on what I wanted and didn't want, I had to determine what I had control over and what I didn't. I had a hard time with this concept because, as a marine, I had been taught instant and willing obedience to orders, and I was required to make things happen with no excuses.

For a civilian, however, it doesn't work like this. Even though you need other people to make things happen, you can't force them. I believe this is what caused my anger. So right away, I knew I couldn't control the actions of others. I let this go and focused on my efforts. I decided I would no longer blame others, the economy, the politicians, or my upbringing for where I was in life. I began to control what I could control: my mind-set. I knew that to get what I wanted in life, I had to find others who lived the life I wanted and do what they were doing. I couldn't be them though; I had to be the best version of me and improve every day. I had to learn how to make a positive impact in the lives of others and be someone people wanted to be around.

First and foremost, I started with a shift in my attitude. I had to ditch the negative, pessimistic attitude and replace it with a positive, optimistic mentality. It started with the content I was putting into my brain. I recognized that garbage in equaled garbage out. I cut out negative people who were dragging me down; if this wasn't possible for all the negative people, I stopped listening to them. I began reading books written by successful people, listening to positive messages, and being more thankful for what I did have versus what I didn't. This shift in my mind-set completely changed my outlook on life. People enjoy being around positive people, and that's whom I wanted in my inner circle. Only cynical people desire to be around negative people; they love being in their unhappy little worlds together.

Every morning, I started my day while lying in bed and thinking only positive thoughts. I made a mental list of a few things I was thankful for and visualized what my day was going to look like. I told myself, "Today is going to be a great day," even if I knew there were going to be some obstacles to overcome. By mentally preparing for the day ahead, I was more likely to have a positive and productive day, even if life decided to punch me in the face, which often happened.

Second, my behavior had to change. I took a hard look in the mirror and saw a man I wouldn't follow based on my behavior; I was immature. I could be the most uplifting and positive person around, but if my conduct was unprofessional, I would have a hard time moving up in life. There's not another person responsible for my behavior; I had to own it. As a former marine, I didn't have a filter. I spoke my mind, often without thinking first, and my mouth had a curse word coming out every other sentence. I began to hold myself accountable for my behavior and attempted to look, act, and speak like the professional I wanted to be, not only at work and in public but in private. Professionalism became a habit.

Last but not least, I knew I had complete control of my effort. My effort was something that had been deep rooted in me since boot camp; I had no choice but to give my all on every task, no matter how small or significant. I had carried over this mind-set to my combat deployments, where a lack of effort could have resulted in lives lost. Again, I had no choice but to give 100 percent to myself, my brothers, and my country. A positive attitude and professional behavior could get me only so far because people would view me as lazy. Successful people don't have time for someone with poor effort, no matter how positive a person he or she is. I had big dreams, but giving half the effort wasn't going to help me achieve those dreams. My effort and energy needed to match my desires. Once I had control of my mind-set and took ownership of my attitude, the words that came out of my mouth, and my effort, I had to dig deep and make significant changes in my personal brand. Once I started to brand myself, many new doors opened for me.

The Man in the Mirror

My mind-set was step one; step two was taking a long, hard look in the mirror. I would catch myself being quick to judge others and was failing to recognize my flaws. For opportunities to present themselves, my integrity needed work; it had to be flawless. The *Merriam-Webster Dictionary* defines *integrity* as a "firm adherence to a code of especially moral or artistic values." In other words, it means always doing the right thing, even when no one is watching. Believe it or not, I've known quite a few people who have poor integrity. One common trait among these people is a pessimistic attitude. They are dissatisfied with life, mainly themselves, and blame everyone else for their problems. These folks are always the victims. I was not going to be the victim.

Integrity was one of the first values taught to me in boot camp. From day one, the drill instructors beat the word and the definition into our skulls. In the Marine Corps, the consequence of poor integrity could cost the lives of fellow marines. As a vehicle commander in the lead LAV, I was responsible for the lives of not only the marines on my vehicle but also the marines in the three other LAVs. My preparation for a mission could save lives or cause a catastrophe. I had to ensure my vehicle had the required maintenance performed, my weapon and the mounted machine guns needed regular cleaning, and I had to know the AO as if I had lived there for twenty years. All of this preparation happened on my own time; no one else could do it for me. And when my lieutenant asked me if I had completed my prepatrol checklist, I could honestly say yes, because I had integrity.

Because I was a prior service member, people respected me. They thanked me for my service and recognized the hard work, dedication, and sacrifice it takes to be a member of the US military. It was vital that I didn't mess this up. I understood I had one chance to make a first impression, and if the impact would be less than favorable, it would tarnish my reputation. It's nearly impossible to recover after that. After the first impression, it was vital that my image remained positive and others viewed me as reliable.

Reliability was never an issue for me. I was always the person who did what I said I was going to do. This stems back to mission accomplishment in the Marine Corps. Getting the job done correctly and on time is crucial to maintaining a solid reputation. When my coworkers noticed I was the guy always following through and performing, one of two things would happen: the pessimists who hated themselves would begin to despise me and talk behind my back and the optimistic group started to seek out my knowledge and skills. I always shared my experience with others because I knew it was essential to be a team player and we were part of a bigger mission—the mission of the company. I avoided the naysayers at all costs and continued to outperform them, and eventually they would leave. I had to be careful though; people often tried to suck me into their gossip. I recognized this was a sure way to tarnish my reputation, and it also showed me whom I needed to avoid. If they were talking bad about someone else, certainly they were talking about me when I walked away. It didn't matter; actually, it motivated me to continue to outperform them. I knew I was good at my job, yet I remained humble.

Humility is a trait that helped me move from one level to the next. There is a fine line between being confident and being arrogant; people are drawn to confidence and repelled by arrogance. I learned how to feel good about my abilities, and instead of bragging about my success, I helped others get the same success. It's a great feeling giving back and assisting others to accomplish more than they usually would have accomplished.

No matter what role I was in, I always strived to be the example. I wanted people to look at my effort, actions, and results and think, *Man, I want to get the results that Jared is getting.* Not only did I try to be the example, I also strived to be kind to everyone, even if they talked down to me or were rude. I knew that if I wanted to continue moving up in life, I had to be a likable person. Whom do people like to be around? They like to be around others who are genuinely kind to them and not fake. They want people in their lives who make them feel good. They want people who work hard and strive not only to improve themselves but to help others develop as well. I learned to have a heart for helping people and found the secret weapon when meeting new people and interviewing: my smile.

Smiling is one of the most powerful weapons, if you are a genuine person. Within the first few seconds of meeting people, they will decide if they like you or not. Your smile creates positive energy, and the other person will naturally smile back. I often sit back and watch the facial expressions of others while I'm at the office; they have an angry look, a neutral look, or a somewhat happy face. It's much easier to say hi to those with happy faces. I have always made it a goal to smile and say hi when I pass someone. If you do this, you'll notice that even if a person has an angry resting face, he or she will look back and smile after a short period of confusion. Be the person who's always upbeat and smiling. This has helped me build the relationships that have led to promotions and new job opportunities.

Of course, smiling can be difficult if we are going through a hard time in life. One of the hardest things I had to learn was how to leave my problems at the door. I learned how to switch on a happy face and perform my duties as usual. Maintaining a positive state of mind and trusting that my issues will eventually pass helped me avoid being distracted by outside problems, which most of the time were out of my control.

CHAPTER

ELEVEN

Shut Up and Listen

O nce you improve yourself inside and out, the next focus is on whom you are spending time with. Your income and level of success are an average of the five people you surround yourself with the most. If your goal is to be a CEO and multimillionaire, then how do you get inside an inner circle of CEOs and executives? You can't just walk up to Warren Buffett and ask him to teach you everything he knows. Well, you could, but it might not work out as planned. I'm sure you can shoot Mark Cuban an email asking for him to mentor you, but you might not get a response. To begin building a network of successful men and women, it starts with finding mentors.

First, decide who and what you'd like to be in ten years, then research and figure out who has achieved that goal and observe them from afar. Follow them on social media, read their books, attend their seminars, watch their body language, pay attention to the way they dress and speak, and learn everything about them. To be successful, it's imperative you do what other successful people are doing.

Second, decide who and what you'd like to be in five years, and repeat the process. This person may be a realistic person to meet and occasionally spend time with. It's essential you create and take advantage of opportunities to spend time around this person and make a positive impression every time you're in the same room. Remember this person may also notice you; you're always on stage, so act like it. When this person is speaking, it's not your time to talk. Shut up and listen so you can learn from the best. Don't forget to always have a pen and journal; don't trust your future to memory.

Third, determine who is in the position you're striving for, maybe one, two, or even three levels above you. Introduce yourself, and explain you're determined to have the success that he or she has accomplished. Compliment this person, and ask if you can schedule a time to sit and chat for thirty minutes once per month. If the answer is yes, your sole focus is to learn everything you can every time you meet. Again, ask a question, and then shut your mouth. Your goal is to build a relationship and also learn the steps this person took to get to where he or she is. Remember to do what successful people do.

There is no limit to the number of mentors you can have, and the mentors you meet with shouldn't last forever because your goal is to eventually mentor them. A great way to network and bump elbows with other high-value people is to join a networking group. These groups are loaded with people focused on making a difference in the lives of others. Step outside your comfort zone as much as you can; the more you do, the more you'll grow.

If you're growing and setting an example as you should

be, others should be seeking you out as well. It's important to remain humble and convey a servant-leader mentality. When others feel you care about them, they are more likely to stay loyal to you and will do anything in their power to support you. When mentoring others, understand it's not just about the mentee learning from you. There's a lot you can learn from everyone, so seek out their experience too.

Choose wisely when letting friends and family into your inner circle. Just because you have known them forever or because they are blood relatives doesn't mean they aren't toxic. Not only will the wrong people try to drag you down with them, but your reputation will suffer. Joel Osteen said, "You can't hang with chickens and expect to soar with eagles." This quote has stuck with me since the first time I heard it. You have to decide who and what you want to be, and you have to surround yourself with those types of people. Transforming from a chicken to an eagle may not be possible; you may have to go from a chicken to a turkey to an owl and then to an eagle. Either way, be cautious with whom you let into your life. Ensure each person is adding some value to you as a person, and you for them.

As you gradually move forward in life, the negative, toxic people will naturally disappear. Stay the course, and the right people will come along.

CHAPTER
TWELVE

Fail Forward

I've stressed over the past few chapters that we are where we are today because of all the decisions we have made up to this point in our lives. For me, I made horrible choices in high school and barely made it through—bottom 10 percent, I'm sure. I decided not to attend college and instead join the US Marines. I decided I was going to give the Marine Corps my all and be the best marine I could be. I decided to leave the marines after four years instead of reenlisting for another four years. I then decided to go to college. When I graduated, I decided to go again and again until I had a bachelor's degree and two master's degrees. I chose that my future was going to be bright, and I was going to build a legacy for my family no matter what it took. Every single decision I have made has been based on one of two things that determined whether I move forward or not: faith or fear.

The sad truth is that fear gets in the way for most people. Often when an obstacle appears or a new opportunity arises, most people make their decisions based on fear. Instead of taking on an obstacle full steam ahead and learning from experience, people avoid obstacles and try to wait them out until they go away. This decision usually backfires and creates a more significant obstacle than it was initially. In America, there are more opportunities than people want to work for, and fear is what makes people avoid opportunity with an unknown outcome. Fear of failure is what holds people back from taking leaps of faith into unfamiliar territory. The comfort zone is the most visited place in the world; it's in the so-called Land of Someday. *"Someday* I'll go back to school." *"Someday* I'll write that book." *"Someday* I'll ask that girl out." Fear is the mayor in the Land of Someday.

This reminds me of the quote by author and motivational speaker Les Brown.

> The graveyard is the richest place on Earth, because it is here that you will find all the hopes and dreams that were never fulfilled, the books that were never written, the songs that were never sung, the inventions that were never shared, the cures that were never discovered, all because someone was too afraid to take that first step, keep with the problem, or determined to carry out their dream.

I genuinely feel I am where I am today and have experienced the success I have today because I dared to punch fear in the face. Each time I overcame an obstacle or took a chance on an opportunity, I became a stronger and wiser person. Each time, our minds adapt and grow. Future obstacles and opportunities no longer seem as stressful; they are more exciting than fearful.

So far in life, I haven't faced an obstacle or opportunity that scared me as much as fighting insurgents in Iraq; however, nothing has ever been as exciting either. As a civilian, when times get tough and I'm faced with a difficult decision, I feel thankful my decision won't cost the lives of others if I'm wrong. If you look at the most successful people in the world, they have failed and have been rejected the most times. On the other hand, others are struggling in life because they've come to their final resting place: their comfort zone. Those who fail and learn from their mistakes will continue to move forward. They must choose to take a chance to make a change. Each time they fail, they fail forward.

Failure has been part of my life since I was a child. Most people don't know this, but I failed the eighth grade. I had to repeat my grade as my friends went on to ninth grade. I was embarrassed and disgusted with myself. Even though I blamed my teachers, it was my fault and my fault only. The following year, my second time around, I earned the best grades I ever had up to that point in school. I decided I was going to put in the effort and do better; I wasn't going to let myself feel like the dumb kid any longer.

One of my most significant failures in life was when I took a leap of faith, quit my job, and started my own business. I had always had a dream to own a supplement store, but fear held me back for many years. While earning my MBA, I wrote a business plan for a possible supplement store, and after presenting the proposal to the class, I felt an urge to follow through and open a storefront. My wife and I had only one child at the time and were in a stable place financially. I couldn't stand my micromanager of a boss and decided enough was enough; I was going to quit and start my business. I kicked fear to the curb and relied on faith to get me through it. I was scared to death; I gave up my stable job with benefits for the entrepreneur lifestyle. Two months and a ton of debt later, the doors finally opened.

We started off with a bang. Our first month was in November, and our sales were hitting all the projections and at times exceeding them. My margins on the products weren't all that good, so my cash flow never really grew. Then summertime hit, and just like every health-and-fitness business, our sales dipped. Over the next four months, our sales dropped lower and lower. It was sweltering outside, and the ancient air conditioner was costing us over $400 a month for our electric bill. I couldn't keep up with the overhead. The cash was dropping fast. Twelve months into the business, I pulled the plug, cut my losses, and closed the doors for good. I loaded a pickup truck and moved $20,000 worth of products into my basement. By far, this was the lowest and most embarrassing moment of my entire life. I was on the verge of giving up, and I was depressed and felt helpless. I felt as if I had failed my wife and daughter. I was lost and didn't know what to do.

I sulked in my sorrows for the next few days. Then one morning, I woke up and decided it was time to take responsibility for my actions and fix the problem. All I could think of was the future of my family. I could feel sorry for myself, or I could get my butt up and make it right. Even though this particular failure was one of the lowest moments of my life, I wouldn't have done it differently. Don't get me wrong: there are many decisions I made while running the business that I would have done differently, but the choice of opening the business helped shape me into the man I am today. Sometimes we need to be punched in the face by life to move forward.

Take chances, and rely on faith that everything will fall

into place. Never hope for the best though. Hoping is like playing the lottery: your odds are low. Rely on your work ethic, and face the fear of failure head on, because when tough times are over, which they will be eventually, you'll see growth. If you quit, however, or never take chances, you'll remain in the Land of Someday. No longer will you let the fear of the unknown or the fear of failure hold you back. Trust yourself, and stay faithful. After all, if you weather the storm, sunshine will soon come.

THIRTEEN

Sacrifice

Why is it that two people graduating high school together with the same God-given talents, the same background, equal education, and the same age can be worlds apart in their careers only ten years later? Many factors come into play, but one thing is for sure: one person maximized his or her time being productive and the other person did not. Since the beginning of time, days have been twenty-four hours long, so why do people assume they don't have enough time in a day? You see, we can't manage time, so it's important to understand that it's up to us to decide how we use the twenty-four hours.

Time is the most valuable asset in our lives; once time passes, we can't get it back. Each day we live, we get closer to the day we die. So if time continues to slip through our fingers, why do we continue to waste it on tasks that aren't helping us improve our current circumstances? Sacrifice is the answer. People are not willing to sacrifice their extra time with tasks that seem like work. I've heard the following time and time again:

- "I don't have time to read."
- "I don't have time to start my own business."
- "I don't have time to exercise."
- "I don't have time to cook."
- "I don't have time to write a book."
- "I don't have time to … "

The excuses pile up, and these people begin to believe their lies. Family legacies are not built during a nine-to-five workweek; ask any millionaire if he or she became wealthy by just going to work, doing the job, and coming home. The answer is "Not a chance."

In the early days of Steve Jobs and Bill Gates, do you think they were out barhopping, playing coed softball, watching *Dirty Dancing* for the umpteenth time, or sleeping until noon? If they had been doing those things, computers and technology wouldn't be where they are today. These two men understood sacrifice; they recognized that the things I just mentioned weren't paying their bills and weren't advancing their careers or businesses. The truth is most people would choose sleep even if they knew that getting up at 5:00 a.m. and working on themselves would set them up for life. Today, people scroll on social media for more than two hours per day; this equates to more than sixty hours each month. What do you think you could accomplish with sixty extra hours per month?

Let's break down a day for an average person, I'll refer to a man since that's what I am, and then I'll break down a day for someone with extraordinary success. The average man will wake up at 7:00 a.m., hit the snooze button five times because he doesn't want to go to work, get his kids ready and drop them off at school, commute for thirty minutes, and arrive at work at 8:00 a.m. on the dot. He'll work a full eight hours doing his assigned duties. After commuting in rush hour traffic, he'll pick up the kids, arrive home at around 5:00 p.m., take care of the kids, eat dinner, relax for a bit, watch some TV, scroll on social media, walk the dog, and talk on the phone. At around 9:00 p.m., after the kids are in bed, he'll take a shower, have a snack, and lie down for bed at around 10:30 p.m. He'll sleep all night, wake up the next day, and do it all over again. Don't get me wrong: this is a comfortable way to make a living and have a peaceful life. However, it's not the life of someone looking to build a legacy.

The extraordinary man's day looks different. He doesn't have special powers, he can't slow down time, and he isn't lucky. He will start the day early and hit the gym at 5:00 a.m. because he knows his health is a priority for success. His workout will be quick and to the point. He'll then rush home, shower, and get ready for the day. He'll read or listen to content that's positive and adds value to his life, all before the kids are awake. After the kids are ready and dropped off at school, he'll arrive at work early because he strives to be the example. Throughout the day, he'll master his craft and learn and practice all he can to be the best at what he does. He'll frequently take on new challenges and step outside his comfort zone. On his drive home, he'll listen to podcasts of successful people in his field or his desired field. When he arrives home, he'll take care of his family, and in the evening, he'll begin working on his side business that pays residual income. Often this may be a direct sales company, side work if this individual is in the trades, or selling a product or service. At the end of the night, the last two tasks he'll accomplish are reading a book that adds value to his life and recapping his day while making a plan for the next day.

As you can see, both of these individuals used their twenty-four hours differently. One man used them to make a living and stay in his comfort zone; the other man used every spare moment to improve. Now don't take this the wrong way; we all need time to unwind and do nothing. It's crucial to our sanity. However, our downtime, leisure, and vacations need to be planned accordingly. Set goals for yourself, and once you achieve them, reward yourself with hockey or concert tickets. Sacrifice now and live later, or live now and sacrifice later. The choice is yours.

My children are my life. I wake up every day and grind because of them. If it weren't for my kids and my wife, I would probably be broke and in a bar somewhere. They are my purpose and my reason; every decision I make or don't make has their best interest at heart. Just like every other family's household in America, ours is loud and sometimes crazy and hectic, especially during the school year. Our two girls are in dance, soccer, and cheer and our youngest is getting to the age where he will be playing sports as well, so soon we will be busy with him. I work a full-time job that requires travel from the west coast to the east coast. My wife and I are both fitness instructors, we run our own direct sales business, and I'm also writing a book. My wife is a member of multiple moms groups and is involved in the church, I play hockey, and we visit the gym twice per week as a family. We are busy, and we love it. Sometimes we complain about it but stop when we realize how blessed we are.

We have a great life; I consider it the American dream. It hasn't always been this way though. My wife and I sacrificed early on in our marriage so things can be the way they are today. My oldest daughter was born while I was still working on my undergraduate degree. I attended school in the morning five days per week, and I worked as a personal trainer before and after class, usually until the late evening. My wife was a school counselor, and we had our baby enrolled in day care. Once I graduated, I began working on my MBA right away, only this time I worked a full-time job during the day and attended school at night. When I was running my business, I worked seven days per week, open to close, for over a year. I then went back to school and earned another master's degree at night while working full time during the day. Sacrifice is hard. It was hard on our family, but because of our hard work and dedication, we are living a life I didn't think was possible in our midthirties.

Understanding what to sacrifice is a skill learned with trial and error. So many people won't take on any new opportunities because they interfere with their kids' sports and activities or even their favorite television shows. They turn down opportunities that could change the trajectory of their lives. Think about it: what can you accomplish while sitting at little Johnny's soccer practice? You can sit and listen to the other moms and dads gossip or brag about how great their kids are, or you can read, make calls to your mentor, or even write that book that you've been putting off for ten years. There's so much wasted time every day that if you take advantage of it, over time you can create massive momentum.

A clear and concise plan of where you're going is crucial to your success. It's impossible to understand what sacrifices you need to make if you're unclear about the end goal. Define your goals and your purpose and reason for achieving your goals. Without a definite purpose, such as building a legacy for your kids, it's easy to quit when times get tough, which they will.

FOURTEEN

Complacency Kills

E very time we lined up our LAVs and locked and loaded our weapons systems for the next mission, we read a sign that stood at our gate where we exited the compound. It was constructed from old plywood and spray-painted to say, "Complacency Kills." The *Merriam-Webster Dictionary* defines *complacency* as "self-satisfaction especially when accompanied by unawareness of actual dangers or deficiencies." In other words, don't get too comfortable with yourself or your environment, for this places you at risk for unknown threats to your well-being. You see, in Iraq, we would go days, weeks, and even months without any contact from the enemy, which created extreme boredom for us, and eventually, we would catch ourselves being complacent. Our level of caution when moving through an unknown area lessened; since nothing was happening, we naturally let our guard down. It seemed that as soon as our guard was down or our sense of security dropped for a moment, we were either hit with an IED or engaged in a firefight. As marines, we were trained to react to the situation instantly. But no matter how much training we received, we all fell victim to complacency at some point in our military careers.

Complacency isn't just a term used for the military; everyone slips into a complacent state of mind sooner or later. Some people can realize they have become complacent and adjust their mind-sets and actions. For instance, a newly married husband and wife have both been gaining weight. They are now in a lifelong relationship and no longer have to impress the opposite sex, so they fall into a comfortable state of mind. After a few months, they notice their jeans are shrinking, and their shirts feel like spandex. So after stepping on the scale, they decide to drop the weight and get back on track with their health. Luckily, they are able to recognize their complacency and refocus their attention.

On the other hand, others may never realize they have fallen victim to complacency. They go through life while "comfortable" and hardly ever have a desire to improve themselves—not only mentally, physically, and financially but spiritually as well. Have you ever noticed when you haven't talked with God recently and then life punches you in the face that suddenly you're God's best friend and begging for his help? The same goes for our mind, body, and finances. Why do people wait until they are near nervous breakdowns to seek help? Why do people let their weight spiral out of control until they feel their only option is weight-loss surgery? Why do people rack up an insurmountable amount of credit card debt before they realize the impact debt has on their lives? It's because all of these people sink into their comfort zones and focus only on the present and how they feel in the moment.

The woman nearing a nervous breakdown doesn't realize it because she occasionally has feelings of being happy and joyful, but she isn't taking action to change her mind-set. The man who continues to gain weight ignores that his clothes are getting tighter; he hides the scale and doesn't look in the mirror. He finds more value in eating than in living a healthy lifestyle. The woman who consistently racks up credit card debt is blinded by the euphoria she feels when buying material goods, which makes her feel on top of the world. Eventually, the world will come crashing down for all three people if they don't realize they are living a complacent lifestyle.

Complacency on a physical level can have an impact on your career if you don't maintain a healthy lifestyle. The first way it will affect your career is through your physical appearance. It's sad, but people still judge books by their covers. If you are interviewing for a job and walk in while looking like your health is on the bottom of your priority list, your chances of getting that job just got smaller. The truth is that even if you are the best in the industry, people have a hard time seeing past your unhealthy appearance. The thought is that if you can't take care of yourself, then how are you going to perform for the company? On top of the physical appearance, medical and pharmacy costs are rising every year; companies are looking to hire qualified people who aren't going to cost them $500,000 a year in medical expenses and missed work. Focus on your three Fs: faith, family, and fitness. Don't let your appearance hurt your chances to show the world how great you are.

Another reason that people get sucked into the complacent mind-set is because of their current circumstances. They sincerely believe that their present circumstances define who they are and who they will become. But this is entirely false! I could name a thousand people who proved this wrong, including me. Have you ever heard of a gentleman named

Tony Robbins, who is an entrepreneur, best-selling author and motivational speaker? A man named Andy Andrews, best-selling author and speaker? How about Eric Thomas, the hip-hop preacher who went from homeless to world renowned motivational speaker? These three people reached a level of personal disgust and made a choice that enough was enough and took responsibility for their lack of action. Often, this level of disgust comes in the form of hitting rock bottom; however, it can also be from hearing or seeing something that gives you hope or changes your belief that your future can be brighter. Once we understand that our current circumstances don't define us, a game plan is crucial for us to move forward and take action.

Once I decided to grab hold of my life and take personal responsibility, around the time my wife was pregnant with our first daughter, a plan of action was essential. Here's an analogy for you: If you want to take a cross-country trip in your car, what would you need to make it successful? First, you would need a destination; a car; and money to keep the gas tank full, to provide food for your belly, and to pay for hotels to stay in. What about a map or GPS? What route will you take? What's your plan if you encounter detours (because you will)? To ensure you don't get too frustrated when obstacles arise, it's important to be prepared and flexible. Your life is very similar; too many people hop in their car of life and take off across the country with no plan, no map, and no money and expect everything to work out. Examine successful people in life. They may not have known where they would end up, but they had a general direction they wanted to go.

As I look back on my life over the past fifteen years, all the dots are finally connecting, and it's because I persevered and made a decision I would leave a legacy for my family. Now from this point forward, I won't be able to connect the dots; it's impossible to know what will happen. However, I know that each dot I create will have a positive impact on my life and the lives of others.

Take a look at your life today compared to five years ago. Are you satisfied with your progress? Did you set goals for yourself, or were you settled into your comfort zone and living in the Land of Someday? For most people, the answer is "No, I'm not where I thought I'd be or where I wanted to be." It's easy to set goals and think about where you'd like to be in five or ten years; you may even make a detailed plan of what you need to accomplish to ensure you achieve these goals. However, one critical factor is missing when turning dreams into a reality is action. Sure, it's all fun and games until we have to get to work, and life continues to knock us down. It's easier to be submissive to life and remain in a position that doesn't cause pain or discomfort. Why do you think people don't exercise? It's uncomfortable, and it hurts at times. But what happens when you start to exercise consistently? Your body begins to adapt, and you develop habits. No longer do you dread going to the gym; instead, you crave your next workout.

Forcing ourselves into action toward our dreams and goals works the same way: you must get comfortable with being uncomfortable. At first, taking action can be miserable. Often we haven't developed the skill, so it's not enjoyable. Our bodies and minds are accustomed to sticking with the status quo and doing nothing above and beyond what is expected to survive. Changing habits and creating new routines take time and accountability. Setting personal expectations from day one and committing in your heart that you will give 100

JARED MCGOWEN

percent of your effort to achieving your goals will ensure that when obstacles arise, you'll blow right through them.

Never settle. Always strive for greatness by moving from one accomplished goal to the next. Yes, you can be content with your life, but to avoid falling into the complacency trap, it's important you always strive for a better version of yourself. What have you wanted to do that you have talked yourself out of over fear or doubt? Have you thought about going back to school? Starting a business? Learning how to play the guitar? How about talking to that pretty woman or handsome man at the gym? Do it! Stop fearing the unknown, and embrace it. Each time you face your fears, you grow and become stronger. The human body and mind are more capable than one thinks, so push yourself far outside your comfort zone; you'll reach the other side a winner.

Remember your current or past circumstances do not define you or your abilities. It's not your fault if you were dealt a lousy hand in life; it is, however, your fault if you die with that same hand.

CONCLUSION

Call to Action

I f you walk away with anything from this book, I hope you apply some of the principles by taking daily action to improve your current circumstances. Successful people make decisions quickly and don't change their minds often; people who fail make decisions slowly and change their minds often. Although this isn't true 100 percent of the time, it has held true for me. I decided to join the marines in about thirty seconds; my gut told me it was the right decision. Did I regret it? Sure, every marine does at some point, but then we get through the rough waters and become the most feared fighters in the world. The major factor is that I committed myself to serve my country; I did it for a more important reason than me. I knew my duty was to write a blank check to the United States of America, payable with my life. Even though I thought about giving up more times than I can count, I never did. I didn't quit because of my purpose and reason for being a marine; the feeling I had while serving my country was stronger than the pain I felt during those times I knew quitting would be the most natural choice.

As you wrap up this book, I want to leave you with a few principles to help you become a better version of yourself. Don't just read these and close the book and move on with your life. Apply these daily. Some days will be harder than others, but remember how you eat an elephant: one bite at a time.

1. Don't bring problems. Bring solutions. Be the person who doesn't complain about all that is wrong but determines a solution and brings it forward. Everyone can recognize there is a problem, and everyone complains. Be the person to resolve it. You'll gain respect and credibility.

2. Make a decision. Stop fearing the decision-making process. Decide. The most successful leaders in the world are those who can make decisions in the most challenging situations. Not making a decision can often be more detrimental than making the wrong decision. Make your decision quickly, and adjust accordingly. Rely on faith versus fear. And most importantly, believe in yourself.

3. Focus only on what is in your control. It's imperative you don't waste your time and energy on things out of your control, specifically the behaviors and actions of other people. Control what you have control of, such as your attitude, behavior, efforts, and actions. Maintain a positive and optimistic mind-set, and be kind to others while always setting the example.

4. Don't expect to soar with eagles if you're hanging around with chickens. Joel Osteen, pastor and best-selling author, said it best. "You'll never meet the right people if you're always hanging around the wrong people." If you have aspirations to improve your life, which you do because you're still reading this book, the people in your life will either build you up or tear you down. Happy people want to be around

other happy people, and successful people want to be around other successful people. You get the picture. Stop spending your time with people who would rather see you fail instead of challenge you to be the best version of yourself.

5. Never stop learning. The beauty of the human brain is that we can acquire an unlimited amount of information; our storage is never full. Have you ever heard the saying "If you don't use it, you'll lose it"? It's true. If you stop trying to learn new things and challenging yourself, you will lose brain power. The good news is that once you decide to stimulate your mind again, it can power right back up—and into high gear. I have never been the smartest, but one thing is for sure: I've always been one of the hardest workers. I've rarely been able to rely on talent to get me by. I have gotten to where I am today by stepping outside my comfort zone by always learning new things, often by trial and error. Always be humble and open-minded to new and sometimes scary ideas.

We have all experienced explosions in life. For me, they were real explosions; for others, these explosions may be different struggles and obstacles in life. Life *will* knock you down. Les Brown said, "When life knocks you down, land on your back because if you can look up, you can get up." We are only one decision away from changing the outcome of our lives, so decide in your heart that you will build a legacy. Each of our legacies will be different. We all have different views of what success looks like, but no matter what, try your best to make a positive impact in this world by finding a way to add value to the lives of other people.

As the marines say, "Semper fi," which means "Always faithful." Be faithful to God, yourself, your family, your country, and those around you, and your life will be blessed and full of happiness.

CPSIA information can be obtained
at www.ICGtesting.com
Printed in the USA
LVHW092022030319
609301LV00006BA/14/P

9 781973 646297